Warrior • 102

The Hitler Youth WITHDRAWN
1933–45

Alan Dearn • Illustrated by Elizabeth Sharp

First published in Great Britain in 2006 by Osprey Publishing,
Midland House, West Way, Botley, Oxford OX2 0PH, UK
443 Park Avenue South, New York, NY 10016, USA
E-mail: info@ospreypublishing.com

A CIP catalogue record for this book is available from the British Library

ISBN-10:1-84176-874-X
ISBN-13:978-1-84176-874-8

Page layout by Ken Vail Graphic Design, Cambridge (kvgd.com)
Index by Alison Worthington
Originated by United Grahics, Singapore
Printed in China through World Print Ltd.

06 07 08 09 10   11 10 9 8 7 6 5 4 3 2

FOR A CATALOGUE OF ALL BOOKS PUBLISHED BY OSPREY MILITARY AND
AVIATION PLEASE CONTACT:

NORTH AMERICA
Osprey Direct, C/o Random House Distribution Center, 400 Hahn Road,
Westminster, MD 21157
E-mail: info@ospreydirect.com

ALL OTHER REGIONS
Osprey Direct UK, P.O. Box 140 Wellingborough, Northants, NN8 2FA, UK
E-mail: info@ospreydirect.co.uk

Buy online at www.ospreypublishing.com

Author's acknowledgements

The author would like to thank Simon Richert and Jo de
Vries at Osprey for their assistance in planning and
preparing this book. Thanks are also due to Ralf Blank from
Hagen Museum for permission to use photographs from his
collection. As ever, I am profoundly grateful to my parents
and to my dear wife Caroline for their unfailing love and
support.

Author's note

The ways in which members of the Nazi youth organizations
became caught up in 'Total War' were extremely diverse, as
were their responses to these experiences. This book
makes use of four composite characters, named Karl,
Maria, Max and Ernst, to give some idea of the different
experiences of German teenagers under the Third Reich.
None of these characters is based directly on a real person,
but all draw upon memoirs and personal testimonies to
provide representative examples of life in the Hitler Youth.

Throughout this book, the English name 'Hitler Youth' is
used to refer to the Nazi Youth organization as a whole.
German titles and abbreviations are used to refer to the four
distinct groups to which German youth belonged, under the
overall leadership of the Hitler Youth. The Deutsches
Jungvolk (DJV) was the Hitler Youth formation for boys aged
between 10 and 14, after which they graduated into the
Hitler Jugend (HJ), or Hitler Youth proper, until the age of
18. Girls aged from 10 to 14 belonged to the Deutsche
Jungmädel (DJM), those from 14 to 18 to the Bund
Deutscher Mädel (BDM).

Artist's note

The artist would like to thank Witham (Specialist Vehicles)
Ltd for their generous help with research for the artwork.
www.witham-sv.com

Readers may care to note that the original paintings from
which the colour plates in this book were prepared are
available for private sale. All reproduction copyright
whatsoever is retained by the Publishers. All enquiries
should be addressed to:

Elizabeth Sharp, Stanton Court, Denton, Grantham,
Lincolnshire NG32 1JT

The Publishers regret that they can enter into no
correspondence upon this matter.

CONTENTS

THE HITLER YOUTH 1933–45

INTRODUCTION

The Hitler Youth was not in essence a military organization. From its origins as the youth department of the brown-shirted Sturmabteilung, or SA, the Hitler Youth expanded to become an all-encompassing institution of the Nazi state. Its purpose was to indoctrinate German children in Nazi ideology, and prepare them physically and ideologically for lives of service to the *Volksgemeinschaft* (national community).

By the outbreak of war in 1939, membership in the Hitler Youth was compulsory for all German children between the ages of 10 and 18. On turning 18, compulsory labour service in the Reichsarbeitsdienst (RAD) took its place, followed by conscription into the armed forces, or Wehrmacht, for the young men. Nazi ideology venerated the soldier as the epitome of the masculine ideal, and it is not surprising that the Hitler Youth was strongly paramilitary in tone from the beginning. Young German men inducted into the Wehrmacht from the Hitler Youth brought with them the skills and attitudes they had learnt there. Following the outbreak of war, the emphasis on pre-military training in the Hitler Youth grew.

Throughout the triumphant years of the 1930s, Hitler Youth groups the length and breadth of Germany had sung their martial songs as they marched, with lyrics like 'the flag means more to us than death' and 'we are born to die for Germany'. These slogans were born in the context of the political struggles of the early 1930s. They may often have been meant metaphorically, but they became descriptive of the experience of members of the Hitler Youth as the war progressed.

Following the disaster at Stalingrad, Joseph Goebbels gave his famous speech at the Berlin Sportpalast on 18 February 1943, in which he called upon the German people to embrace 'Total War'. For young German children, 'Total

A Hitler Youth models the recently introduced winter uniform in 1938. On his upper left shoulder he wears the *Gebietsdreieck*, identifying him as belonging to the Berlin *Gebiet* of *Obergebiet Ost* (east). (Ullstein)

War' meant that they found themselves increasingly mobilized for actual participation in combat. From February 1943, 15- and 16-year-olds came to bear the brunt of manning the air defences of the Reich as *Luftwaffenhelfer* (air force auxiliaries). The year 1943 also saw the creation of the 'Hitler Jugend' Division, under the aegis of the Waffen-SS, but recruited from senior members and recent graduates of the Hitler Youth. As the 12th SS-Panzer Division, this unit fought savagely against British and Canadian troops around Caen after the D-Day landings, and was largely destroyed in the process. From late 1944 units of Hitler Youth were directly used in combat as part of the people's militia, the Volkssturm. In the final months of the war, Allied soldiers regularly encountered armed children in battle, including boys as young as ten and girls from the Bund Deutscher Mädel.

Often the most determined resistance encountered by Commonwealth and US troops in the last months of the war came from groups of Hitler Youth. These 14–15-year-olds were captured near Münster at the beginning of April 1945. According to the original caption, they only surrendered after using up their ammunition, and remained 'arrogant'. (IWM EA 61636)

CHRONOLOGY

1922
19 March Gustav Lenk advertises the formation of a youth arm of the National Socialist Party in the party newspaper, the *Völkischer Beobachter.*

1926
27 July The Hitler Youth officially established under the name Hitler Jugend, Bund der Deutschen Arbeiterjugend. This became part of the SA, under the leadership of Kurt Gruber.

1930
Hitler Youth disrupts screenings of *All Quiet on the Western Front* throughout Germany. Film banned as a result.
July The Nazi organization for girls, which had existed since 1927, formally named the Bund Deutscher Mädel.

1931
30 October Baldur von Schirach appointed *Reichsjugendführer* at age 24.

1932
26 January 12-year-old Hitler Youth Herbert Norkus killed in street fight with Communists in Berlin. Commemorated as Hitler Youth martyr in the movie *Hitlerjunge Quex*, 1933.
July, November Hitler Youth active in lead-up to Reichstag elections.
October 100,000 members of the Hitler Youth attend a mass rally at Potsdam.

1933
30 January Hitler appointed Chancellor.
3 April Hitler Youth takes over Reich Committee of German Youth Associations. Other youth associations (apart from Catholic groups) abolished or absorbed.
17 June Schirach becomes *Jugendführer des Deutsches Reiches.* All youth groups and activities come under his control.

1934

30 June 'Night of the Long Knives'. Ernst Röhm and leadership of the SA purged.

1935

1 March Hitler reintroduces conscription in Germany, in defiance of the Treaty of Versailles. Labour service in the RAD for 18-year-old boys becomes compulsory in June.

1936

1 December Law concerning the Hitler Youth. Membership of the Hitler Youth made theoretically compulsory. Catholic youth organizations closed down.

From 1937

Paramilitary training in the Hitler Youth intensifies, in cooperation with the Wehrmacht and SS.

1939

1 September Germans invade Poland. Outbreak of Second World War.

1940

8 August Artur Axmann takes over from Schirach as *Jugendführer*. Schirach retains the position of 'Delegate for the Inspection of the Whole of the Hitler Youth'.

26 September Hitler orders Schirach to organize the *Kinderlandverschickung* evacuation programme.

1942

13 March Establishment of *Wehrertüchtigungslager* military training camps for the Hitler Youth.

1943

January Destruction of the German 6th Army at Stalingrad.

25 January Hitler authorizes the conscription of Hitler Youth as anti-aircraft auxiliaries.

24 June Formation of 'Hitler Jugend' Division. Officially named '12th SS-Panzer Division "Hitler Jugend"' on 30 October.

1944

6 June British, Canadian and US troops land in Normandy.

22 June Opening of Soviet offensive against German Army Group Centre.

20 July Unsuccessful attempt to assassinate Hitler.

August Remnants of 'Hitler Jugend' Division largely destroyed in the Falaise Pocket.

25 September Creation of the Volkssturm people's militia, consisting of those aged 16–60.

16 December Germans launch offensive in the Ardennes (the 'Battle of the Bulge').

1945

8 February Breslau encircled by Soviet troops.

27 February Hitler sanctions the recruitment of 15–16-year-olds, at Himmler's request.

5 March Conscription of those born in 1929.

7 March US troops cross the Rhine at Remagen.

25 March Nazi 'Werewolves' assassinate the US-appointed mayor of Aachen, Dr Franz Oppenhoff.

28 March Axmann announces the formation of Hitler Youth anti-tank units in the *Völkischer Beobachter*.

16–17 April Soviet troops cross the Oder and capture the Seelow Heights, the last major obstacles before Berlin.

20 April Hitler's last birthday. Soviet attack on Berlin begins.

25 April Encirclement of Berlin complete. Soviet and US troops meet on the Elbe.

30 April Soviets have by this stage reached central Berlin. Suicide of Hitler.

2 May General Weidling surrenders Berlin.

3 May Hamburg surrenders to the British.

6 May Breslau surrenders to the Soviets.

7 May Formal surrender of German armed forces at Rheims.

The 12th SS-Panzer Division 'Hitler Jugend' was a direct product of Hitler Youth indoctrination and training. Thrown into action against British and Canadian troops in June 1944, it performed far more effectively than many on both sides had predicted. These young *Panzergrenadiers* of the division are receiving medals less than two weeks after the D-Day landings. (Ullstein)

JOINING THE HITLER YOUTH

Max was born in Rothenburg ob der Tauber, near Nuremberg, in 1920. Joining the Deutsches Jungvolk (DJV) was for him the most natural thing in the world. His parents had been enthusiastic supporters of the Nazi Party since the mid-1920s, his father joining the SA in 1926. From a young age, Max had witnessed demonstrations and marches in which his father took part. He sometimes joined with other local boys in marching alongside the ranks of Brownshirts, singing their songs. He longed to be old enough to wear a uniform of his own and march behind the swastika banner. It was a proud moment for him and his parents when he was inducted into the DJV on 20 April 1930, on Adolf Hitler's birthday.

From *Kampfzeit* to *Gleichshaltung*

For Karl and Maria, born in 1928, and Ernst, born in 1929, the experience of joining the Hitler Youth was very different. Max had joined the DJV during the *Kampfzeit* – the 'time of struggle' – when the Nazi Party was still battling for supremacy both in the Reichstag, and frequently in the streets. Karl, Maria and Ernst grew up in a Germany transformed after Hitler's appointment as Chancellor in January 1933. As part of what the Nazis euphemistically called the *Gleichschaltung* ('coordination') of all aspects of German society, the young people of the Reich came under the control of the Hitler Youth. The title of Baldur von Schirach, leader of the Hitler Youth, changed ominously from 'Reich Youth Leader of the NSDAP [National Socialist German Workers' Party]' to 'Youth Leader of the German Reich' on 17 June 1933. Less than a month later, the 'Reichs Committee of German Youth Associations' was abolished. This effectively brought the many pre-Nazi youth organizations in Germany under Schirach's control, which invariably meant their abolition or absorption into the Hitler Youth.

The Hitler Youth often played a prominent role in the pageantry of the Third Reich, which gave many members a sense of being involved in something grand and exciting. Here BDM and HJ line a triumphal arch to welcome German motorcycle troops. (Author's collection)

The first to go were the Communist and other left-leaning youth groups of Weimar Germany. In the case of religious youth organizations, Schirach was obliged to tread more carefully. Protestant youth groups presented little problem, with many voluntarily joining the Hitler Youth. This was formalized in December 1933, after which all members under 18 were integrated into the Hitler Youth. In practice, this could have confusing consequences. Henry Metelmann was a member of the Protestant *Christian Jungschar* in Hamburg in 1934. At one meeting, he was surprised to find his group joined by a procession of Hitler Youth, with whom they marched off to the local HJ headquarters. When they arrived, they were told that they had now joined the HJ, much to the consternation of Henry's staunchly left-wing parents.

Catholic youth groups held on more tenaciously to their autonomy, but were finally absorbed by the Hitler Youth in December 1936. A law passed at that time made membership of the Hitler Youth theoretically compulsory, although this was enforced more effectively with the *Jugenddienstpflicht* (Youth Service Duty) law of 25 March 1939. This legally compelled any German girls or boys between the ages of 10 and 18 who were not already in the Hitler Youth to join. However, as late as November 1942, a further law reinforcing police sanctions against those not joining the Hitler Youth shows that the *Jugenddienstpflicht* was not completely successful in its aims.

Maria and Ernst turned ten in 1938 and 1939 respectively. They looked forward to joining the DJM and the DJV as a tangible sign that they were growing up. At last they could join the grown-up world of their older siblings and friends, with its smart uniforms and exciting activities like hiking and camping. As far as their parents were concerned, joining the Hitler Youth was simply what that was. Things were a little more difficult for Karl, growing up in a staunchly Catholic family in Dortmund. Karl was the first of his siblings not to follow their father and grandfather into the Catholic Youth Movement, which had been absorbed into the Hitler Youth after 1936. His parents objected to what they called the 'pagan trappings' of the Deutsches Jungvolk, but Karl was excited to be joining his schoolmates in their new brown shirts.

Children a few years older than Karl from similar backgrounds often faced difficult choices in the years after 1933. Although the Hitler Youth was technically voluntary until 1936, children often faced enormous pressure from peers and Nazi teachers to conform. It was not unusual for students who had not joined to receive extra homework, to be humiliated in class, and to be set tasks such as to write an essay on the

Hiking and camping played a prominent role in the Hitler Youth, and many members found these activities very appealing. Here a *Pimpf* of the DJV is dropped off at a camp by his family. (Author's collection)

topic of 'Why I am not in the Hitler Youth'. Violent clashes between the Hitler Youth and rival organizations were also not uncommon. More damaging for many young people who remained outside the Hitler Youth during the 1930s was the sense that they were out of step with the exciting transformation of Germany going on around them. For example, such feelings led Melita Maschmann, who was to become the head of the press department of the BDM by the war's end, to join the organization secretly in 1933, against the wishes of her parents.

Induction

The Nazi Youth Leadership consciously sought to promote the induction ceremonies of the Hitler Youth as rites of passage comparable to, and ideally as replacements for, religious rituals such as Confirmation. Every year, on Hitler's birthday (20 April), a solemn ceremony was held at Marienburg Castle, once the headquarters of the Teutonic Knights. This was broadcast around Germany, and incorporated into the hundreds of local induction ceremonies. The sense of being part of a great quasi-medieval rite occurring throughout Germany was often a very moving experience for those undergoing it. Alfons Heck, who was inducted into the DJV in 1938, recalls that '... my spine tingled in the conviction that I now belonged to something both majestic and threatened by bitter enemies'.

Swearing an oath of allegiance to Hitler formed the focus of the ceremonies. One set of guidelines given to Hitler Youth leaders in Trier in 1940 stressed that

> For everybody the hour of his induction must be a great experience. The *Pimpf* [DJV boy] and *Jungmädel* [DJM girl] must regard this hour of their first vow to the Führer as the holiest of their whole life.

Boys transferring from the DJV to the HJ took the following oath:

> I swear that I will serve the Führer Adolf Hitler faithfully and selflessly in the Hitler Jugend. I swear that I will always strive for the unity and comradeship of German youth. I swear obedience to the Reich Youth Leader and to all leaders of the Hitler Jugend. I swear on our holy flag that I will always be worthy of it, so help me God.

Organization

The boy or girl newly inducted into the Hitler Youth became a member of a unit organized along military lines. Membership in a particular group was determined geographically, with boys or girls from the same area or street being grouped together, rather than by school classes. In the big cities in particular, children often knew nobody from their original groups. When Ernst, a native of Berlin, transferred from the DJV to the HJ at the age of 14 in 1943, he was assigned to a *Kameradschaft* with nine other boys. Four *Kameradschaften* made up a *Schar*, four *Scharen* a *Gefolgschaft*. Between three and five *Gefolgschaften* made up a *Stamm*, the administrative control area of which was called an *Unterbann*. Four or five *Unterbanne* together formed a *Bann*, with around 40 *Banne* belonging to a *Gebiet*, an administrative area corresponding to a *Gau* of the NSDAP. The triangular patch worn by all members of the Hitler Youth on their upper left shoulder identified the *Gebiet* to which they belonged. This appeared under the name of one of the six *Obergebiete* in the Greater German Reich – *Nord, Süd, West, Ost, Mitte* and *Südost* after the *Anschluss* with Austria in 1938. For example, Ernst's patch bore the title *Ost – Berlin* in two lines. All four branches of the Hitler Youth were organized along similar lines, although the names of units varied. For example, the BDM equivalents of the HJ *Kameradschaft, Schar* and *Gefolgschaft* were named *Mädelschaft, Mädel-Schar* and *Mädel-Gruppe* respectively.

From Hitler Youth to military service

The Hitler Youth was intended to control the lives of young Germans from the age of 10 to 18. The reintroduction of conscription in 1935 brought with it the additional expectation that boys would fulfil nine months of labour service in the Reichsarbeitsdienst (RAD) before their military service. The pre-military training undertaken by the Hitler Youth even before the war made those who had been through the movement attractive candidates for recruitment. As a result, different Party and military organizations competed for access to and control over the best products of the HJ, in an example of the wasteful empire building and competition that were endemic in the Third Reich.

From its formation in 1922 until the mid-1930s, the Hitler Youth operated as the junior SA, and was essentially under its control. This relationship between the Hitler Youth and the SA was severed following the purge of the SA in June 1934, known as 'the Night of the Long Knives'. The separation was formalized by an executive order of 29 March 1935, which established the Hitler Youth as a distinct organization of the Nazi Party alongside the SA and SS.

Competition between the SS and Wehrmacht

With the control of the SA over the Hitler Youth removed, competition heightened between the Wehrmacht and SS for its best recruits. The

After turning 18, graduates of the Hitler Youth had to undertake labour service. These young recruits pose outside their work camp hut in the brown uniforms of the RAD. (Stavka)

relationship between the SS and the Hitler Youth was encouraged as early as 1934 by the creation of the *HJ-Streifendienst* (Patrol Service), the security wing of the HJ, which formed close ties with the SS and Gestapo. Former members of the *Streifendienst* were obvious candidates for recruitment into the Gestapo and the SS-Totenkopfverbände, the formations that furnished the guards for concentration camps. By the end of 1938 the SS were also actively recruiting from the *HJ-Landdienst* (Land Service), as part of a programme envisaged by Himmler to create soldier-farmers for the colonization of conquered territories in Eastern Europe.

An even more direct challenge to the Wehrmacht's prerogative in recruiting the cream of the HJ was posed by the creation of the SS-Verfügungstruppe (SS-VT), or 'Special Duty Troops', with the reintroduction of conscription in March 1935. Service in the Waffen-SS, as the SS-VT units were generally known by spring 1940, was attractive to many HJ in the early stages of the war. For example, Max joined the Waffen-SS in 1940 after his RAD service, attracted by the sense that he was joining an elite brotherhood. Others found the high standards of the SS intimidating, or were repelled by the hostility towards church affiliation that was typical of its members. It also became widely known that the formidable reputation the Waffen-SS won in battle was achieved at the cost of significantly higher casualties than were suffered in other units.

Competition was fierce between the Waffen-SS and the Wehrmacht for the best recruits from the HJ, and, as the war progressed, for any recruits at all. With the successive drop in the age of conscription during the war, recruits increasingly moved from the HJ straight into the armed forces, bypassing the RAD. The call-up age in 1940 was 19, dropping to 17 in 1943. In autumn 1944, a major attempt was made to recruit voluntarily those boys born in 1928, the remainder of whom were conscripted in February 1945. Finally, those born in 1929 were conscripted by a directive of 5 March 1945. Hitler responded with 'pride

Two young soldiers from a Waffen-SS unit surrender to US troops in Northern Alsace, January 1945. Allied troops tended to regard such boys as 'fanatics', but many members of the Hitler Youth ended up in the Waffen-SS after being pressured to 'volunteer'. (IWM SF10A)

1

and joy' in a proclamation of 7 October 1944 to the registration of the class of 1928 as *Kriegsfreiwillige* (war volunteers), citing their 'unshakeable will to victory' that had been already demonstrated in combat.

Part of this demonstration had been provided by the recent combat employment of the 12th SS-Panzer Division 'Hitler Jugend' against the British and Canadians in Normandy. In February 1943, following the Stalingrad debacle, an agreement had been struck between Schirach's successor as *Reichsjugendführer* Artur Axmann and the SS recruitment chief Gottlob Berger to raise a division from the HJ. Volunteers were sought from 16- and 17-year-old boys born in the first half of 1926, who had their requirements for RAD service waived. The division was formed around a cadre of experienced NCOs and officers, many drawn from the Leibstandarte SS-'Adolf Hitler' (LAH) division. By the time the Allies invaded Normandy on 6 June 1944, the so-called 'Baby Division' had become a fully equipped and well-trained Panzer division.

During the war, therefore, the purpose of the Hitler Youth organizations for boys changed from providing pre-military training to becoming a pool of 'manpower' that could be tapped directly for use in combat. Max turned 18 in 1938, completed his service in the RAD, and joined the SS in 1939. In contrast, Ernst, born in Berlin in 1929, became eligible for conscription in March 1945, two months before his 16th birthday. In the final year of the war, members of the Hitler Youth became particularly vulnerable to recruitment by local Party or military authorities, especially when already concentrated in training camps or evacuation centres away from parental scrutiny. For example, despite no longer being *Reichsjugendführer*, Schirach was made responsible in September 1940 for organizing the *Kinderlandverschickung* (KLV). The KLV was an evacuation programme, intended to remove German children from cities at risk of air attack. Once in camps away from home and parents, the children often found themselves called upon to perform labour tasks such as digging anti-tank ditches and, in the final stages of the war, as recruits for the armed forces. Reinhold Kerstan was a 13-year-old boy in 1945, evacuated from

An interesting photograph that seems to depict a very young soldier leaving for the front. The grenades ready to hand in the soldiers' belts suggest that contact with the enemy is possible. (Stavka)

Berlin to a KLV camp in Czechoslovakia. One day, his entire school year were pronounced old enough to join the HJ, as a special 'honour', and immediately taken out to train with rifles and grenades.

The Volkssturm

Above all, it was under the umbrella of the Volkssturm ('People's Assault') that children fought as soldiers during the final months of the war. This militia was established by Hitler's decree on 25 September 1944, and mobilized all men born between 1884 and 1928 who were not otherwise engaged in military service. Anyone serving in a RAD camp was liable for immediate conscription into the Volkssturm, as were boys in KLV camps. As a direct consequence of the July 1944 bomb plot against Hitler, the Volkssturm was placed not under Wehrmacht control, but under the more 'reliable' command of members of the Nazi Party hierarchy. Martin Bormann was responsible for the recruitment and organization of the Volkssturm, through the administrative control of his *Gauleiters*, or district leaders, while the actual military employment and command of the Volkssturm came under the command of Heinrich Himmler, as Commander in Chief of the Home Army.

The Volkssturm provided the SS with an excellent means of recruiting members of the HJ directly into the ranks of the Waffen-SS. For example, Armin Lehmann, who acted as Artur Axmann's messenger during the battle for Berlin, belonged to a unit of HJ within the Volkssturm that was inducted as a whole into the Waffen-SS. Despite being issued with SS pay books, the boys never underwent their medical examination, and thus never received the SS tattoo indicating their blood types. This may have saved some of the boys' lives when captured by the Red Army. Another former HJ within the Volkssturm tells of his unit being forced to stand to attention for eight hours in March 1945 until they 'volunteered' for the SS. Those few who refused to succumb to this pressure were derided as 'Christians' by the recruiters, and warned to keep silent about their experience. Wehrmacht recruiters criticized SS methods such as these as 'the categorical demand to join voluntarily'.

After his training at a military preparation camp in January 1945, Ernst received orders to report for induction into the Berlin Volkssturm. He was required to kit himself out with an appropriate uniform, boots and a rucksack, and joined a motley crowd of HJ boys and old men for a swearing-in ceremony. German troops called Volkssturm units 'casseroles', because they were made up of old meat and young vegetables. However, as was often the case, Ernst and his HJ unit formed a distinct company within the Volkssturm. This partly reflected the fact that boys from the HJ were already organized into groups when drafted into the Volkssturm, but was also testimony to their generally higher morale and greater familiarity with weapons. One HJ leader put in charge of organizing the Volkssturm near Luxemburg in 1945 remembers the contrast between the poorly motivated old men and the Hitler Youth boys, who saw themselves as an elite. Artur Axmann took this trend further in January 1945 by obtaining Hitler's permission to set up distinct HJ tank hunting brigades under his own command as *Reichsjugendführer*. Many of the boys of 14 or even younger who were thrown into combat during 1945 belonged to such units, often raised by local Hitler youth leaders in the face of imminent enemy attacks.

The *Flakhelfer*

Although 15-year-olds were officially conscripted into the armed forces in 1945, many other German boys of the same age had been engaged in frequent and harrowing combat experiences from spring 1943 as anti-aircraft auxiliaries. As with the formation of the 'Hitler Jugend' Division, the enlistment of members of the HJ and later BDM into the Flak defences was a response to the catastrophic defeat at Stalingrad. In early 1943, Göring obtained the reluctant permission of Bernhard Rust, the Reichs Education Minister, to allow the Luftwaffe to conscript auxiliaries from German schools.

Under the provisions of this law, whole classes of schoolboys aged between 15 and 17 were enlisted in the Luftwaffe. Flak auxiliaries were liable to indefinite service, theoretically proceeding into the RAD and the Wehrmacht when they turned 18. Despite initial assurances that the boys would be stationed close to their homes, they were often moved about in response to the changing military situation, with most being sent to Berlin, Hamburg, the Ruhr or the Baltic Coast. By the end of the war, about 200,000 German teenagers had served in this way. The auxiliaries called up in this manner were officially known as Luftwaffenhelfer-Hitler Jugend (LwH-HJ), which was shortened to *Luftwaffenhelfer*, or *Luftwaffenhelferin* in the case of women. Although the name was unofficial, *Luftwaffenhelfer* were ubiquitously referred to as *Flakhelfer*. Our composite character Karl, born in 1928, was called up as a *Flakhelfer* along with the rest of his class in March 1944.

Entire school classes were drafted into the anti-aircraft defences as *Luftwaffenhelfer*. Here a class from the Hohenlimburg grammar school is handed over to a Luftwaffe NCO by its teacher in March 1943. (Ralf Blank, Hagen)

The BDM

Nazi ideology emphasized the life of the soldier as the natural destiny of a man. In contrast, the idea of women bearing arms was abhorrent to Hitler personally, and totally counter to the value the Nazis placed on women as passive child bearers and housewives. Nevertheless, from 1940 women were called up to serve in auxiliary contexts such as clerical posts and communications. Senior graduates of the BDM and RAD were conscripted as *Helferinnen* into the army, navy, Luftwaffe and SS. By 1945, there were approximately half a million *Wehrmachtshelferinnen*. Although they were officially forbidden to take part in combat, this prohibition was often unrealistic given the contexts in which *Wehrmachtshelferinnnen* served. For example, service in the occupied territories left them open to partisan attack.

Members of the BDM were never officially conscripted into serving in the Flak defences in the way that members of the HJ were. Nevertheless, it was not unusual by 1944 for detachments of *Luftwaffenhelferinnen* to be augmented by 17- and 18-year-old girls drawn from the RAD, or 16- and 17-year-olds from the BDM. Usually, these young women were responsible for crewing searchlights, fire control and sound detection equipment. However, by the end of the war it was not unknown for *Luftwaffenhelferinnen* to be crewing the Flak guns themselves. In either case, Nazi ideology never reconciled itself to the employment of women in such martial roles. For example, training for *Luftwaffenhelferinnen* encouraged young women to think of their barracks as a home, thus maintaining the official position that the role of women belonged in the domestic sphere. Similarly, when some young women were trained in the use of Flak artillery in 1945, this was not officially acknowledged. Their identification papers only described them as 'ZBV' ('For Special Use').

Werewolf

A final way in which children of the Hitler Youth became combatants at the end of the war was as Werewolves. The Werewolf organization was

Female *Luftwaffenhelferinnen* like this crew of a 150cm searchlight in the Ruhr in autumn 1944 were supposed to be recruited from young women over the age of 18. Nevertheless, many members of the BDM joined their ranks by the end of the war. (Ralf Blank, Hagen)

originally envisaged by Himmler in November 1944 as a guerrilla force, charged with sabotage and raids behind the lines of the advancing Allies. *Gauleiters* were to suggest suitable recruits, who were trained at secret locations in the Rhineland and Berlin. The most important training centre in the west was at Hülchrath castle, near the Rhenish town of Erkelenz, which in early 1945 was training around 200 recruits. Most of these were drawn from the Hitler Youth.

The most famous achievement of the Werewolves was the assassination of Dr Franz Oppenhoff, whom the US Army had installed as the mayor of occupied Aachen. A Werewolf commando of five men and one woman was dropped by parachute from a captured US B-17 behind Allied lines on 20 March 1945. The youngest of them was a 16-year-old boy named Erich Morgenschweiss. The Werewolves achieved their aim on 25 March, gunning down Oppenhoff outside his home.

Numerous other acts of sabotage and murder were undertaken by small groups of SS-trained Werewolves as late as July 1945. However, Goebbels used the assassination of Oppenhoff as propaganda for wholesale resistance against the Allies in occupied Germany. Many sporadic acts of resistance were carried out by members of the Hitler Youth and others who considered themselves to be Werewolves, in line with Goebbels' propaganda, but who had nothing to do with the actual Werewolf organization. For example, in the face of imminent capture by US troops, one German officer commanding a unit of HJ asked for volunteers to fight on with him as Werewolves. When only one boy stepped forward, the officer decided that he might as well surrender after all.

TRAINING

At the outbreak of the Second World War, there were probably no other teenagers in the world as well prepared for military service as the youth of Germany. The society that Max, Karl and Ernst grew up in during the 1930s intensively socialized them for their future role as soldiers. Hitler laid down his ideal for the youth of Germany in a speech at the Nuremberg Party Rally in September 1935: 'In our eyes the German youth of the future must be slim and slender, swift as the greyhound, tough as leather, and hard as Krupp steel.'

In line with this ideal, physical games and activities were the main focus of the Hitler Youth. This was emphasized from the moment a boy joined the DJV as a ten-year-old *Pimpf*. For the first six months of Max, Ernst and Karl's time in the DJV, they were on probation. Under the supervision of older boys they prepared for the exacting *Pimpfenprobe* test that would allow them to become full members of the organization. This instruction by older boys was in keeping with Schirach's mantra for the Hitler Youth, that 'youth must be led by youth'. To pass the *Pimpfenprobe*, each of the boys had to be able to run 60 metres (just over 65 yards) in 12 seconds, throw a ball 25 metres (approximately 27 yards), perform a long jump of 2.5 metres (2¾ yards) and take part in a hike of up to several days, as well as learning key Hitler Youth songs and slogans. Finally, they also had to undertake a *Mutprobe* (courage test). In Karl's case, this required him to leap over the parapet of a

second-storey building, without being able to see whether older boys were ready to catch him in a tarpaulin. Only after passing all these tests were the boys entitled to wear the full uniform of the DJV, including the coveted Hitler Youth dagger.

The emphasis on competitive physical challenges continued throughout a boy's experience of the Hitler Youth. Sports such as athletics, football, discus and especially combative sports such as boxing were undertaken by all members of the DJV and HJ, and were organized into annual competitions at local and regional levels. Hiking and camping were also widely practised. One insidious result of the focus on aggressive competition in the Hitler Youth was that despising weakness was actively encouraged. Those who could not reach the exacting physical standards required were often treated brutally. For example, non-swimmers were sometimes 'taught' to swim by being thrown into a deep pool, and only rescued when on the point of drowning. Atrocities committed against prisoners by the German armed forces, such as the execution of Canadian prisoners by elements of the 'Hitler Jugend' Division in Normandy, owed much to the brutalizing effect of such training.

Of particular use as pre-military training were the popular 'terrain games'. These activities formed one of Karl's happiest memories of his time in the Hitler Youth. A typical game involved Karl with the nine other boys of his *Kameradschaft* spending a day in a forest attempting to locate the headquarters of a rival group. When they discovered it, their goal was to remove their opponents' flag. Each of the boys wore woollen threads around their arms, indicating their 'lives'. When they inevitably clashed with the boys from the 'enemy' group, the day of creeping through the forest climaxed in a free-for-all scuffle to tear off the 'lives' of their opponents. Through these games, German boys from a young age learned skills of field craft, map reading and camouflage, as well as attitudes of aggression, which would prove useful to many of them in the Wehrmacht.

In addition to the emphasis on physical training, special units of the HJ were formed to offer training specific to different branches of the armed forces. In 1933 the *Motor-HJ* had been formed, which catered to

Despite never having the resources it needed, the *Motor-HJ* provided valuable training for future soldiers in the mechanized units of the Wehrmacht. Members wore a distinctive and practical uniform of overalls and crash helmet. (Ullstein)

members of the Hitler Youth with particular interests in motor vehicles. With the increasing focus on military training after 1937, this trend towards specialization within the Hitler Youth continued. The *Flieger-HJ* was formed in 1937 to provide training for future Luftwaffe cadets. Its members learnt the rudiments of practical flying in gliders, as well as skills such as navigation. Close links were often formed between the boys of *Flieger-HJ* units and the personnel of nearby Luftwaffe airfields. The *Marine-HJ* offered specialized maritime training as preparation for the navy, while other smaller specialized units of the DJV and HJ focused on military skills such as horsemanship, signalling and air-raid defence.

Conscription reintroduced

After conscription was reintroduced on 16 March 1935, overt military training became a more pronounced aspect of life in the Hitler Youth.

Drill and marksmanship with air rifles and small-calibre firearms had been among the activities of the DJV and HJ since the late 1920s. However, from 1935 the Wehrmacht and SS began to furnish the HJ with resources and instructors to provide pre-military training, and sought to secure the best recruits for their formations. In 1937, the then Lieutenant-Colonel Erwin Rommel played a leading role in establishing formal liaison between the army and the HJ, although his attempts to bring the HJ under army control were strenuously resisted by Schirach. This closer relationship had significant consequences for Max, who had risen through the ranks to lead a *Gefolgschaft* of 160 boys in his final year in the HJ during 1937–38. He was now able to make use of expert army instructors to teach his boys marksmanship and field craft, and able to arrange interesting visits to army facilities. Throughout Germany, the

result of this relationship between the army and the HJ was reflected in the rising standard of marksmanship within the youth organization. By early 1939, 1.5 million boys were training regularly on rifle ranges under Wehrmacht supervision, and 51,500 boys had won the prestigious HJ marksmanship medal.

For Max personally, a more important development was the strengthening relationship between the HJ and the SS. Realizing the potential recruitment opportunities, Himmler began furnishing the HJ with trainers drawn from the ranks of the SS from 1936. This direct competition with the Wehrmacht bore fruit in Max's case. His contact with SS trainers during 1937 and 1938 impressed him greatly, and was responsible for his decision to join the motorized infantry regiment 'Leibstandarte SS-"Adolf Hitler"' in 1939, after completing his labour service in the RAD.

After the outbreak of war, the role of the HJ in providing pre-military training for the armed forces became even more apparent. By 1940, members of the HJ were expected to spend four hours every week in 'defence readiness' activities such as marksmanship and field exercises based on those in the infantry training manual, with an additional six hours every month to be devoted to sports. In an ominous development, the leadership of the HJ changed the name of its 'Office for Physical Education' to that of 'Military Training' in January 1941, in an attempt to coordinate the pre-military training of the HJ more effectively.

The leadership of the Hitler Youth during the war sought to revive in German children the sense of urgent duty that had characterized the movement prior to 1933. Once again, German youth were living through a 'time of struggle', and their duty was to prepare themselves for the important work to which the Führer was calling them. For German boys, this of course meant the work of soldiers, and the leadership of the Hitler Youth spent considerable resources in glamorizing the armed forces as an exciting life to be keenly anticipated. One example of this was the 'Front soldiers speak to the HJ' programme, which organized exciting talks by soldiers who were on home leave or recuperating from wounds.

Until paper shortages in 1943 curtailed their production, German boys were also bombarded with publications glamorizing the prowess of the German military, and especially its prestige arms such as the U-Boats, Stukas and Panzers. As the Nazi leadership increasingly looked to the youth of Germany, publications produced by the Hitler Youth deliberately emphasized the military responsibilities of younger and younger children. One example of this is

Magazines like *Der Pimpf*, published by the Hitler Youth, helped to glorify the life of the soldier. In this issue from 1943, boys as young as 14 were told that they were already men, and encouraged to look forward to military service. (Author's collection)

Freundlein

Der Pimpf

Wer
14 ist, ist schon ein Mann
*
Mann im Winter
*
Die Gebirgswiese
*
Der Teufel ist los

NATIONALSOZIALISTISCHE JUNGENBLÄTTER
BERLIN • NOVEMBER/DEZEMBER 1943 • FOLGE 11/12 • PREIS RM. 0,20

found in the July/August 1943 edition of *Der Pimpf*, a magazine aimed at members of the DJV. The magazine begins with a full-page dedication, stressing that in light of the total war in which Germany was engaged, 'he who is 14 is already a man'. Publications such as these appealed powerfully to the desire felt by many adolescents for a sense of significance and purpose, especially as they themselves suffered the loss of family members or experienced the horrors of air attack. Another magazine published jointly by the army and the Youth Leadership in May 1943 challenged its young readers to aspire to the heroism being shown by German troops. Written in response to the defeat of the Wehrmacht in Tunisia, a series of stirring stories concludes with an appeal to the 'youth of the Führer' to recapture Africa once again.

The *Wehrertüchtigungslager*

By the beginning of 1942, the rigours of war on the Eastern Front were felt to require the expansion of training facilities for the HJ. A decree from Hitler on 13 March 1942 authorized the establishment of *Wehrertüchtigungslager der Hitler-Jugend* throughout the Reich. The purpose of the *Wehrertüchtigungslager* (literally 'military service competency camps') was to provide 16–18-year-old members of the HJ

Boys of the HJ arrive at a *Wehrertüchtigungslager* in December 1944. Within a couple of months, many of them would be committed to battle. (Ullstein)

with a concentrated infantry-training course over three weeks. The boys were expected to use their annual holidays from school or work to attend the training. By the end of 1943, 226 of these camps had been set up, servicing 515,000 HJ. The camps were run by HJ leaders who held Wehrmacht officer ranks, working in conjunction with training personnel drawn from the Wehrmacht or the Waffen-SS. Predictably, the Waffen-SS saw the *Wehrertüchtigungslager* as presenting a golden opportunity to poach the best recruits, and used their good relationship with *Reichsjugendführer* Artur Axmann to have as high a profile in the camps as possible. By 1943, no fewer than 42 of the camps were staffed by Waffen-SS instructors, an impressive achievement given that the Waffen-SS only comprised about 5 per cent of the total manpower of the armed forces.

As Karl was conscripted as a *Flakhelfer* in March 1944, shortly before his 16th birthday, he was not expected to receive training in a *Wehrertüchtigungslager*. In contrast, Ernst received a letter summoning him to attend training in January 1945, despite being only 15. The trainers at the *Wehrertüchtigungslager* Ernst attended outside Berlin were experienced NCOs drawn from the Waffen-SS. Some of them – the better ones – were soldiers seconded to training while recuperating from wounds. However, there was a distinct group of NCOs at the camp who had been rejected by the field divisions for various reasons. These instructors were often embittered, and prone to taking out their frustrations on the boys in their charge.

Each of the three weeks Ernst attended the camp was dominated by a slogan, in turn 'We Fight', 'We Sacrifice' and 'We Triumph'. The boys

The original intention of the *Wehrertüchtigungslager* was to provide realistic military training in an attractive way. Providing instructors who could act as role models was one way of achieving this. In this posed photo from March 1943, a highly decorated *Hauptmann* explains tactics to admiring HJ through the use of a sand table. (Ullstein)

received a great deal of ideological training revolving around these slogans, the point of which was to portray violent struggle as their natural and glorious contribution to the destiny of the German *Volk*. While at the *Wehrertüchtigungslager*, Ernst was also trained in the use of high-powered weapons such as the Mauser 98K carbine, the MG42, grenades and the *Panzerfaust*. It was the *Panzerfaust* above all that offered the leadership of the Hitler Youth the opportunity to deploy often extremely young children in combat. The weapon fired a hollow-charge projectile capable of destroying the heaviest tanks of the Soviets and Western Allies. It was relatively easy to use, was cheap to manufacture, and was recoilless, which meant that even a ten-year-old could use one, whereas the recoil of a rifle or machine gun would knock him flat.

Ernst hated almost every minute of his time at the *Wehrertüchtigungslager*. The few exceptions were mealtimes, at which Ernst and his comrades were treated with abundant and good food, to the extent that Ernst gained weight during his time at the camp despite the physical exertion. The instructors placed considerable pressure on the boys to join the Waffen-SS,

In the *Wehrertüchtigungslager*, boys from the HJ undertook many activities familiar from the Hitler Youth, but with their military purpose made clear. The popular 'terrain games' now became reconnaissance training, under the eyes of experienced military personnel. (Ullstein)

although they received some measure of protection from the Hitler Youth leaders of the camp. In Ernst's case, he had taken the precaution suggested by an older friend of pre-registering with an army unit, which he was due to join after his HJ and RAD service. Ernst's experience of the petty brutality of some of the SS instructors simply confirmed the bad opinion he already had of the organization.

Training the 'Baby Division'

The training of the 'Hitler Jugend' Division was distinct from that of other Wehrmacht and Waffen-SS formations, and reflected many of the core values of the Hitler Youth. In particular, the idea that youth must be led by youth was reflected in the relatively young age of the cadre of former HJ members who provided many of the officers and NCOs of the division. For example, Max was called back from service with the Leibstandarte Division to take command of a company in the 25th Panzergrenadier Regiment of the 'Hitler Jugend' Division at the age of only 23. Even the commanders of the Division were relatively young, with the original commander Fritz Witt being aged 34 at the time of his death in 1944, while his replacement, Kurt Meyer, was only 33. The youth of the division as a whole was reflected in the fact that its members were issued with a ration of sweets instead of cigarettes, much to their disgust. Although he had few qualms about throwing German

Panzergrenadiers of the 12th SS-Panzer Division 'Hitler Jugend', the nearest carrying the highly effective MG42 light machine gun, prepare for a counterattack in Normandy, June 1944. In the background stands a Pz.V Panther, probably belonging to the Division's 12th SS-Panzer Regiment. (Ullstein)

children into battle, Himmler remained concerned to the end that they not learn the habit of smoking.

Max joined the recruits of the 'Hitler Jugend' Division at their training facility at Beverloo in Belgium in August 1943. The boys he trained had come straight from various *Wehrertüchtigungslager*, and were fit and highly motivated. They looked up to Max, the experienced veteran of the Eastern Front, as a model to emulate and impress. Training at Beverloo reflected the comparative egalitarianism of the Hitler Youth ethos. Max was encouraged to develop a close relationship with his 'men', and he took pains to explain the purpose of orders rather than expecting unthinking obedience. In this way, the military unit itself was supposed to mirror the ideal of the *Volksgemeinschaft*. Little emphasis was placed on drill, training instead aiming to give as realistic an idea of actual battle as possible. The 'terrain games' of the Hitler Youth supplied the model for this, with boys of the Hitler Jugend training intensively in exciting and demanding field exercises.

Training for the BDM

Girls of the BDM officially received no formal military training. Throughout its history, the BDM downplayed military activities for its members. Equal emphasis was placed on physical fitness for girls as for boys, but its purpose was completely different. Sports for boys tended to emphasize individual achievement and competition. Activities such as rhythmic gymnastics for girls placed emphasis on group play and identity, and were supposed to give visual expression to the idea of the *Volksgemeinschaft*. Above all, German girls were supposed to be fit and healthy to supply the Reich with healthy children. Germans came up with various disrespectful acronyms for the initials 'BDM' that reflected its purpose, such as *Bald Deutsche Mutter* ('Soon a German Mother'), *Bedarfartikel Deutscher Männer* ('Requisites for German Men') and *Bubi Drück Mich* ('Squeeze Me, Baby!').

As a result of these attitudes, when Martin Bormann suggested the formation of a battalion made up entirely of women in early 1945, Jutta Rüdiger, the head of the BDM, energetically opposed him. In the final months of the war, Rüdiger did authorize BDM leaders to receive training in the use of pistols for self-defence, but she remained committed to the idea that bearing arms was contrary to the biologically determined nature of women as caregivers and nurturers. Nevertheless, many young women throughout Germany did find ways to receive military training. This was usually done at their own initiative, and with the ad hoc support of local HJ or Volkssturm units. Many German girls were unhappy with their official non-combatant roles. For example, one woman from the Rhineland who was 14 in 1945 remembers being trained in the use of the *Panzerfaust*, and longing to get at the enemies who had been bombing her homeland for years.

Inefficiencies of training

Despite all the efforts made by the leadership of the Third Reich to ensure that young men received the maximum pre-military training

The *Volksgemeinschaft* in action. Girls of the BDM give an athletics display, designed to reflect the organic unity of the German people. Their outfits were considered quite risqué at the time. (Ullstein)

possible, the endemic factionalism of the Nazi bureaucracy meant that this was done in a deeply inefficient manner. In the HJ, the *Wehrertüchtigungslager*, the RAD and finally the armed forces, young recruits were taught and re-taught drill with no attempt to coordinate this instruction between the different services. This was often extremely frustrating for HJ leaders who had taught drill sometimes to hundreds of younger boys, only to have their skills treated with contempt by instructors in the RAD and Wehrmacht.

It is also important to note that many of the avenues intended to provide members of the HJ with training were overstretched to the point of collapse by the end of the war. Many young boys were thrown into combat with inadequate training. For example, when Karl was drafted into the Volkssturm from service in the Flak in March 1945, he was almost entirely unprepared for his new role as an infantryman. *Luftwaffenhelfer* provided an obvious reservoir of 'manpower' to be used in ground combat once they were no longer needed in the Flak defences, but most of them had never gone through even the basic infantry training of the *Wehrertüchtigungslager*. Instead, Karl was rushed through a mere four days of weapons training at a *Wehrertüchtigungslager* before being thrown into battle against US troops, and his experience was by no means unusual.

EVERYDAY LIFE IN THE HITLER YOUTH

Education

Schirach's goal from 1933 was to bring the whole lives of the young people of Germany under the control of the Hitler Youth. One significant problem for this aim was how to reconcile it with the traditional institutions of German education, which continued to make the greatest demands on the time of German children until at least the age of 15. Hitler's personal failure at school contributed to a marked attitude of anti-intellectualism in the Third Reich, which caused conflict between the schools and the Hitler Youth to the detriment of the traditionally high standards of German schooling.

When Hitler became Chancellor in 1933, Max was one of a small number of children in his class who belonged to the DJV. When he left his *Hauptschule* (non-selective high school) two years later at 15 to take up an apprenticeship, this had changed dramatically, with more and more of his peers joining the Hitler Youth. Nazi triumphalism in the early 1930s, coupled with the anti-intellectualism of the Party leadership, caused considerable friction between the Hitler Youth and their teachers. Embracing the dictum that youth ought to be led by youth, leaders in the Hitler Youth were encouraged to reject the 'bourgeois' authority of their teachers, as well as the traditional curriculum and teaching methods. It was not unknown for this rejection of school authority to result in actual physical attacks upon teachers by HJ students, and clearly the licence given to youth could be used to settle all sorts of perceived wrongs suffered at the hands of their teachers. In one case in 1933, a Latin mistress in Munich who was notorious for giving low marks had all the windows of her flat broken by a group of HJ.

In the face of mounting complaints from parents and teachers, the ineffectual Minister for Science and Education, Dr Bernhard Rust, attempted to reach an accord with the HJ. From July 1934, Saturdays were designated as the *Staatsjugendtag* (State Youth Day), and were kept free of homework for members of the Hitler Youth. Sundays were supposedly preserved for the family, although Hitler Youth activities often encroached on this time. In 1934 an agreement was also reached between Rust and Schirach to appoint a Hitler Youth *Schuljugendwalter* (School Youth Warden) to adjudicate disputes between the Hitler Youth and the school. At the same time, Rust's wholesale replacement of Jewish, left-wing or otherwise 'unacceptable' teaching staff from 1933 with members of the National Socialist Teachers' League, as well as the wholesale 'Nazification' of the school syllabus, brought schools more into step with the aims of the Hitler Youth.

Education under the Nazis reflected their obsession with 'racial purity'. Here, students at an elite NAPOLA receive instruction in the scientific basis for hereditary illness. (Ullstein)

Karl was an academically accomplished student, and passed selection to attend a *Gymnasium* (selective grammar school). Since Rust had shortened the time students were expected to remain at school by a year in 1938, Karl had expected to sit for his *Abitur* school-leaving examinations at the age of 17 in 1945, although his service as a *Flakhelfer* and then in the Volkssturm were to make this impossible. After a decade of Nazification, the standard of education was so low, and so dominated by ideological training, that many qualifications were not recognized in post-war Germany. Karl and Maria, who attended a girls' secondary school, received many lessons on proper racial attitudes, which in Maria's school centred on the themes of their responsibility as German women to keep the precious blood of the *Volk* unpolluted by 'un-German' influence, epitomized above all by the Jews. No subject was untainted by the insidious influence of Nazi ideology, with even mathematics being taught in such a way as to instil Nazi values in the young. For example, Karl and Maria both used a textbook that contained this question: 'The construction of a lunatic asylum costs 6 million RM. How many houses at 15,000 RM each could have been built for that amount?'

A logical consequence of the Nazi disdain for traditional education was the establishment in 1937 of a new type of school, the *Adolf Hitler Schulen* (AHS). These schools were placed under the jurisdiction of the Hitler Youth, rather than Rust's education ministry. By the end of 1943 there were 12 of these schools, catering for 2,027 students. Their aim was to provide the future political and administrative elite of the Third Reich, and they reflected the values of the HJ in stressing the importance of physical achievement over academic excellence. Only one-and-a-half hours per day were allocated to lessons, most of which were concerned with ideological topics, in comparison to the five hours each day devoted to sports and physical activities. The major achievement of the AHS was to sink the level of German educational standards to a new nadir.

Somewhat more successful were the *Nationalpolitische Erziehungsanstalten*, or NAPOLAs, which had similar aims to the AHS in seeking to provide the future elite of the Reich. In characteristic fashion, the NAPOLAs, of which there were 21 by 1940, were controlled by the SS in competition with the AHS. NAPOLA students maintained only nominal ties to the Hitler Youth. The aim of the NAPOLAs was to turn out 'political soldiers', whom they produced by immersing their students in a regimen of drill, reinforced by often-brutal physical challenges. The individual identities of the students were suppressed, and group hazing of those who did not fit in was encouraged. That being said, the NAPOLAs did succeed in achieving much higher academic standards than those of the AHS. The approach to education also anticipated the sort of training that recruits in the 'Hitler Jugend' Division were to receive in 1943–44, with informal relations between teachers and students encouraged.

Pressures of service

Another reason for declining education standards in the Reich, additional to Nazi interference with the curriculum and teaching standards, was that students were often exhausted from all the extra

Hitler Youth duties they were expected to perform. The concept of *Dienst*, or 'service' for the *Volk*, was central to Hitler Youth ideology, and made up an increasingly heavy burden on youth under the pressures of the war.

Even before the war, members of the Hitler Youth were expected to perform a wide range of 'services', the most obvious of which was attendance at the bi-weekly Hitler Youth meetings. These were officially held on Wednesday evenings and Saturday afternoons. Saturday afternoons were set aside for sport and outdoor activities. Wednesday evening was the so-called *Heimabend* (home evening), when the Hitler Youth unit met at their *Heim*, or clubhouse. From 18 July 1934, a weekly radio programme called 'The Hour of the Young Nation' was broadcast to coincide with these evenings. The decoration of one's *Heim* was often a source of pride and competition within the Hitler Youth, with HJ units seeking to outdo each other by finding secret or exotic locations for their clubhouse, and decorating it with posters, flags and militaria. Max was able to make use of his father's SA connections to set up his *Kameradschaft's Heim* in the cellar of a pub, to the envy of many of his friends.

Former members of the Hitler Youth often have very different memories of their *Heim* evenings, and their enjoyment of them often depended on the ability of their leaders to inspire interest or come up with exciting activities. Ernst, for example, enjoyed the Wednesday evenings he spent with his *Kameradschaft* engaged in activities such as model-making, or listening to inspiring war and adventure stories told by his leader, a gifted storyteller. Maria's experience was not so positive. She found the evenings tedious, dominated as they were by learning songs and 'women's' skills such as needlework, in which she had little interest. Her group leader also insisted on giving her girls political instruction, although these sessions usually involved her merely reading out material supplied by the BDM, rather than allowing lively discussion.

For some children, Hitler Youth meetings proved to be so objectionable that they sought ways to avoid them. The *Jugenddienstpflicht* (Youth Service Duty) law of March 1939 had laid down sanctions against those avoiding Hitler Youth Service, sanctions that were reinforced by law in November 1942. Nevertheless, it sometimes remained possible to avoid meetings, especially in the larger cities once the Anglo-American bomber offensive began to disrupt urban life seriously.

Landdienst

From 1934, assistance with harvest work and other agricultural tasks, known generally as *Landdienst* (Land Service) became an important part of the Hitler Youth's activities. By 1942 this had become compulsory, and was of enormous benefit to the German economy. In that year, 600,000 boys and 1.4 million girls were sent off for six weeks during their summer holidays to bring in the harvest. However, in addition to its economic value, Hitler Youth *Landdienst* also often had the more sinister purpose of promoting the imperialistic aims of the Reich.

This was perhaps particularly true in the case of the BDM. From 5 January 1938, all girls in the BDM were required to fulfil a *Pflichtjahr* (Duty Year) after the age of 16, and before their service in the RAD. In keeping with Nazi ideas about the role of women, this 'duty' was to take the form of either domestic or agricultural work. After the conquest of

Czechoslovakia, Poland and France in 1938–40, a considerable number of girls from the BDM either volunteered or were sent as part of their *Pflichtjahr* to newly conquered regions. There they helped prepare for the colonization of these areas by ethnically German settlers. The example of this on the largest scale was the wholesale repopulation of the Warthegau – formerly Polish territory around the southern tip of Upper Silesia – with *Volksdeutschen* (ethnic Germans). About a million Poles were dispossessed from their land as part of this process, which involved 19,000 girls from the BDM in 160 camps assisting in the preparation of Polish farms and villages for German settlers.

Such *Osteinsatz* (eastern employment) often came as a profound shock for girls from cosmopolitan cities like Berlin, Leipzig or Dresden, as they found themselves attempting to teach hygiene and even the German language to peasants who were practically indistinguishable from the Poles they were supplanting. For example, Melita Maschmann writes of her experience leading girls of the BDM in a RAD camp in the Warthegau. Despite the idealism with which she approached the work of expanding the frontiers of the Reich, she found the experience of trying to share her enthusiasm with superstitious East Prussian *Volksdeutschen* deeply frustrating. Such was her belief in the need for Germany to expand its borders that she recalls feeling no compassion for the Poles, even when she was directly involved in helping a unit of SS evict the inhabitants of a village.

HJ enjoy a relaxed moment during their *Landdienst* agricultural service. They are standing outside their *Heim* (barracks), the sign on the wall of which identifies the group as belonging to *Gebiet* 23, from the Middle Elbe. (Ullstein)

A recent graduate from the BDM holds the baby of some happy *Volksdeutsch* farmers in a propaganda photograph from 1940. In reality, many idealistic members of the BDM and RAD sent to work in Nazi colonies like the Warthegau found their experiences deeply disillusioning. (Ullstein)

In general, girls of the BDM experienced a more radical change to their daily lives as a result of the outbreak of war than did boys of the HJ. The emphasis on pre-war 'service' in the DJM and BDM was on preparing German girls to become docile and effective helpers to men, mothers and homemakers. Whereas RAD service had been made compulsory for boys along with conscription in 1935, it was only made compulsory for girls after the outbreak of war in 1939. To some extent, this could still be justified in the Nazi mind as an opportunity for young German women to learn domestic skills suitable for their future role as wives and mothers, even if by the end of the war their labour was often used in such decidedly non-domestic tasks as digging anti-tank defences. The pretence became harder to sustain after 1941, with the need for workers in the war industries leading to graduates of the BDM being expected to perform six months each of RAD service and *Kriegshilfsdienst* (War Assistance Service), often in armaments factories.

Kriegseinsatz

At the outbreak of war in September 1939, Schirach called upon the Hitler Youth to make its own contribution to victory. As a result, increasingly heavy demands were placed upon its members to engage in *Kriegseinsatz* (war employment). Some tasks, such as involvement in the *Landdienst* and collecting money for the Winter Relief appeal, were already part of Hitler Youth life before 1939. However, the outbreak of the war saw the whole emphasis of the Hitler Youth shift away from ideological instruction and sport towards their use in the war economy, which would culminate in the boys at least being viewed as soldiers by 1945.

Members of the Hitler Youth were called on to fulfil a range of duties, over which their parents and schools had little control. As a *Pimpf* of the DJV in Berlin in 1940–42, Ernst spent many of his afternoons after school along with the other boys of his *Jungenschaft*

Pimpfe of the DJV collect clothing for Winter Relief, 1937. After the outbreak of war, boys like these, as well as girls of the DJM and BDM, were kept busy collecting a wide range of scrap for use in the war effort. (Ullstein)

collecting material for the war effort. It made him feel that he was really helping Germany win the war to knock on apartment doors in his uniform and ask whether the household had any clothing, or scrap paper, or scrap metal that it could spare. He and his friends even collected old bones, which were used to manufacture explosives. Girls from the DJM and the BDM were mobilized to scour forests and fields for mushrooms, herbs and flowers for the production of teas and pharmaceuticals.

Boys and girls of the Hitler Youth were also called upon to take over jobs previously held by adults. Members of the HJ and BDM performed a myriad of roles in order to free up men for the front, including tram conductors, road workers, postmen, telephonists and clerks. For example, during the first year of the war 64,000 BDM girls worked for the German Red Cross, 60,000 more were caring for the wounded in military hospitals, 11,000 were engaged in clerical duties for the police, 1,500 were working for emergency fire departments, and up to 100,000 were working in railway stations.

From 1942, one of the most common uses of the Hitler Youth was in the *Luftschutz* (air defence) of the Reich. This involved a range of duties. For example, many major cities had fire-fighting squads made up of members of the HJ. As a boy of 13 in Hamburg in 1943, one former Hitler Youth acted as a messenger stationed at an air-raid bunker. In the case of the telephone system being knocked out, his job was to run messages from one shelter to another, even during air raids. He performed this duty in addition to the six hours every day he spent at school, his Hitler Youth service twice a week, and afternoons spent collecting scrap. Along with many of his peers, he was brought face to face with the horror of war from a young age, being required to help with the stacking of bodies after raids. Girls from the DJM and BDM were also often employed in *Katastropheneinsatz* (disaster action) duties, feeding and assisting the homeless and shocked after air raids.

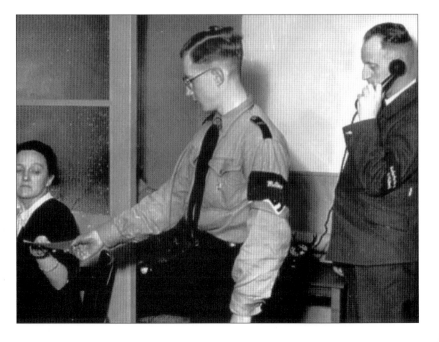

Runners from the DJV and HJ were regularly called upon to deliver messages when communications were disrupted by air raids. This *Melder* (messenger) from the HJ wears an armband identifying his role. (Ralf Blank, Hagen)

A: HJ sports, summer 1938

B: Training in a *Wehrertüchtigungslager*, January 1945

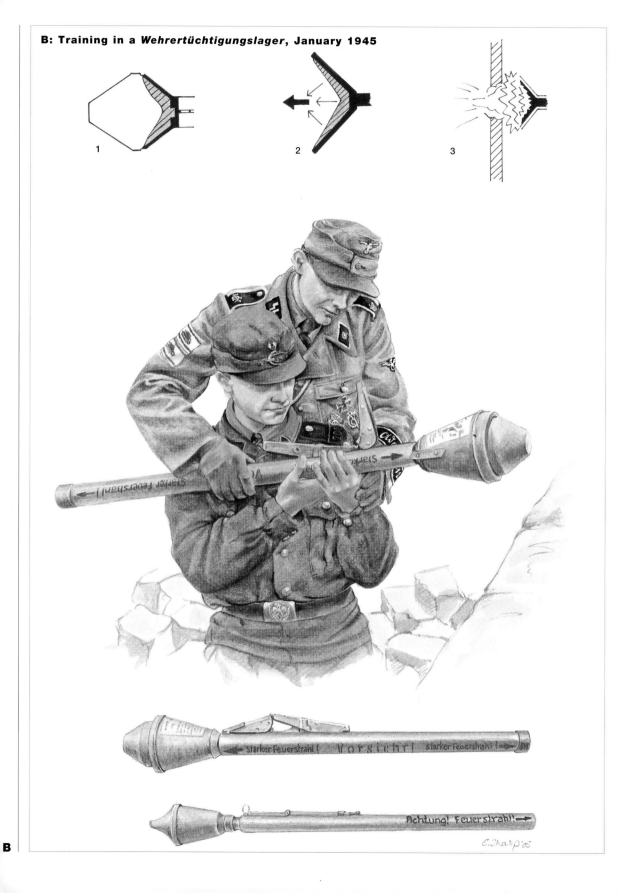

1

2

3

starker Feuerstrahl!

starker Feuerstrahl! Vorsicht! starker Feuerstrahl!

Achtung! Feuerstrahl!

C.Sharp'05

C: *Luftwaffenhelfer* at a Flak installation, March 1944

D: BDM girls join a searchlight crew near Berlin, autumn 1944

E: Hitler Youth in the *Luftschutz*, Köln, 1943

F: The HJ Division counterattacks near Caen, June 1944

G: Child soldiers in the Volkssturm, Ruhr pocket, April 1945

KLV

Another way in which young Germans found themselves entrusted with heavy responsibilities was through the *Kinderlandverschickung* (KLV) programme. The KLV was originally conceived in 1934 as a way of allowing urban children in poor health to spend time in the healthy air of the countryside. In 1941, the scheme was transformed into an evacuation programme, under Schirach's direction, to enable children aged 10–16 to escape cities threatened with air attack. This was particularly appealing to some within the leadership of the Hitler Youth, as it provided the opportunity to gain complete control over the education of the children, separated as they were from parental and school supervision. Many parents recognized this fact, but their reluctance to allow their children to come under the control of the KLV was balanced against the danger of their staying in the cities, and the fact that whole schools were evacuated at the same time. Children who stayed behind were left without their friends or access to education.

By 1944, there were 3,500 KLV camps throughout the Greater German Reich, and 800,000 children had passed through them. Many of the leadership duties within these camps fell to senior members of the HJ and BDM. For example, it was not unheard of for a girl of 16 to be the director of a camp holding 130 girls between the ages of 10 and 13. This was part of a general trend within the Hitler Youth as a whole, in which younger and younger members held leadership positions during the war, as older members were conscripted to military duties. Having been indoctrinated with Hitler Youth values such as contempt for weakness from an early age, the young leaders at KLV camps instituted regimes that were often severe. Children who wet their beds, for example, were often harshly 'disciplined', with beatings or other punishments. In one camp, minor misdemeanours were punished by locking the child in a smoke house, used for curing ham, until they passed out. The young leaders of such KLV camps were also often faced with the problem of dealing with a hostile local population around the camp. As with the *Landdienst*, KLV camps were often located in conquered territories as a form of colonization. It was not unknown for children staying in the camps to be attacked, especially in the face of the looming German defeat in 1944–45.

The Hitler Youth presented authorities with an easily tapped and usually willing labour force. They were commonly called upon to assist with the dangerous work of clearing up after air raids, as is the case with these *Pimpfen* of the DJV, photographed in Stettin in 1943. (Ullstein)

As the frontiers of the Reich contracted, the Hitler Youth were often involved in the demanding welfare work of assisting refugees and displaced people. Here HJ and BDM distribute newspapers to refugees arriving from the east in late 1944. (Stavka)

Flakhelfer

The 15- and 16-year-old boys drafted into the Flak defences as *Luftwaffenhelfer* from early 1943 found themselves living a strange pseudo-adulthood. Officially, they remained members of the HJ, and were supposed to

continue receiving school instruction. *Gymnasium* students like Karl, for example, were supposed to receive 18 hours of lessons each week, half their normal school load. Lessons were to be taught by the boys' regular teachers, who were expected to travel to the Flak positions and give instruction to their students at the site. HJ service also remained an expectation placed upon the young *Flakhelfer*. As late as September 1944, the leadership of the Hitler Youth was urging regional leaders to make a greater effort to visit the boys at their emplacements, and to ensure that normal HJ activities such as drill, sports and marksmanship training were still being done.

These expectations were completely unrealistic, and stemmed from the fiction the Nazi leadership sought to maintain that *Luftwaffenhelfer* were auxiliaries or cadets rather than actual combatants. Under the pressure of attacks by the RAF at night and the USAAF during the day, maintaining any pretence of school lessons usually fell by the wayside. Even when an attack was not imminent, the boys were often exhausted and in shock after combating the RAF until 2–3am, and in no mood for Latin or Geography. Their teachers were also often unable or unwilling to make the sometimes-dangerous journey to the Flak emplacements, especially since most of them by 1943 were old men called out of retirement to replace those conscripted for the front.

The attempts by the Hitler Youth to maintain control over the *Flakhelfer* were also unsuccessful. As will be discussed further below, the ambiguous position *Flakhelfer* occupied between the HJ and the Wehrmacht – and between childhood and adulthood – often resulted in them holding a distinct sense of their own identity. Boys who were continually putting their lives at risk and operating powerful weaponry saw themselves as soldiers, not as members of the HJ. *Flakhelfer* usually resisted attempts by local HJ leaders to reassert their authority over them, often with the support of their Luftwaffe commanders.

Daily life for the *Flakhelfer* was dominated by the routines of the emplacement where they were stationed. Frequent drill was a chore to be endured, especially given the considerable experience most had brought with them from the DJV and HJ. Karl, serving with a heavy Flak unit near Aachen in 1944, was luckier than many of his peers in that his

A crew of *Flakhelfer* commanded by a Luftwaffe NCO mans a 20mm Flak 38 anti-aircraft gun near Hagen-Haspe in February 1944. (Ralf Blank, Hagen)

Flakhelfer often spent much of their time on labour tasks, repairing or maintaining their installations. This group, photographed in September 1943, seems to be building a concrete-lined shelter. They wear Luftwaffe fatigue uniforms with their *Luftwaffenhelfer* caps. (Author's collection)

battery commander, a Luftwaffe Oberleutnant, allowed the boys under his command a reasonable degree of freedom from unnecessary military rules. Karl's regular station at the battery was with the fire control equipment. This position, known as B1, held an Em 4m R40 stereoscopic range finder, connected to a *Kommandogerät 40* fire control computer, which together directed the fire of the battery's six 88mm Flak guns. When not on duty, Karl spent much of his time in the barracks hut he shared with seven other boys, smoking, playing cards and talking about girls. The boys had been able to decorate their hut much as they pleased, their NCO even turning a blind eye to a risqué pin-up Karl had attached to the inside of his cupboard door. One of Karl's friends had improvised an electric hotplate, on which they supplemented their diet with fried potatoes and leeks 'organized' from nearby fields. On occasion, as a small act of rebellion, Karl even exchanged a few words or a cigarette with one of the Russian POWs who acted as ammunition bearers for the battery.

When it was possible, the part of Karl's week he looked forward to most was weekend leave. This provided him and his friends with a taste of the adult freedoms that their position as *Flakhelfer* made possible. Wearing their uniforms with the HJ insignia removed, the boys were able to use the small amount of money they received for their duties to engage in activities otherwise forbidden for boys of their age. These included staying late in pubs, smoking, and going to the movies. Since March 1940, a national curfew for those under 18 had barred young people from restaurants and pubs after 9pm, and youths under 16 were entirely banned from these places and cinemas unless accompanied by an adult.

UNIFORMS AND APPEARANCE

The members of the newly created youth arm of the NSDAP after 1922 modelled their appearance on that of the SA. This was a source of some

The point of the game is no longer clear, but these *Flakhelfer*, photographed in July 1944, are enjoying the moment. (Author's collection)

BOTTOM LEFT **According to Baldur von Schirach at his trial in Nuremberg, the uniforms of the Hitler Youth were supposed to promote equality, not militarism. Here the summer and winter uniforms are seen together. (Stavka)**

BOTTOM RIGHT **In practice, adhering to uniform regulations was often preserved for official parades and propaganda photos. The boy on the right wears the correct M1937 winter uniform, but seems to have misplaced his armband, while his friend wears a decidedly non-regulation jumper. (Stavka)**

friction between the two organizations. After Kurt Gruber was appointed *Reichsführer* of youth in July 1926, a concerted effort was made to standardize the uniforms of the Hitler Youth, and to differentiate them from those of the SA.

The basic uniform for boys of the HJ changed little between the mid-1930s and the end of the war. The summer uniform theoretically consisted of a brown shirt, black shorts, and long brown or grey socks. A black scarf was worn around the neck, and a black belt with regulation HJ buckle. Headgear consisted of a brown side cap, replacing an earlier peaked cap, which bore a diamond-shaped HJ badge at the front. The M37 winter uniform consisted of very dark blue-black trousers and waist-length blouse, worn over a brown shirt with black scarf. The blue-black peaked M35 field service cap was worn with the winter uniform. The

same insignia was worn with both the summer and winter uniform, the most striking feature of which was the swastika armband, worn on the upper left arm. In deliberate contrast to the armband of the SA, this featured a black swastika within a white diamond, the red armband divided in two by a white stripe.

Girls of the DJM and BDM wore a white blouse with a navy blue skirt. On transferring to the BDM, the 14-year-old girl was given a black scarf, worn under the collar and fastened with a plaited leather woggle. In cooler months, a brown imitation suede jacket with four pockets was worn over this basic uniform, nicknamed an *Affenhaut* ('monkey skin'). A diamond-shaped Hitler Youth patch was worn on the left sleeve. The popular uniform was completed with black shoes, white ankle socks and a navy-blue cap or black beret. Both boys and girls were expected to supply their own uniforms, which could have embarrassing consequences. For example, one former member of the BDM remembers having to wear a navy skirt made by her mother, which was not nearly as smart as the ones bought in shops. Henry Metelmann's Socialist father refused to buy him the brown shirts he needed for the HJ, resulting in two shirts being given to Henry by the Party as a hardship case.

Uniforms worn by the 10–14-year-old *Pimpfen* of the DJV were similar to those of the HJ, with some distinctive differences. For example, *Pimpfen* often wore shorts with their winter uniforms. Most notably, members of the DJ did not wear the HJ armband, instead wearing a circular black patch on their upper left arm, which bore a single *Sig* rune. This distinctive insignia was a reminder of the fact that the DJV had a separate origin to that of the HJ, originating amongst Austrian and Sudeten Germans, before it was absorbed into the HJ during the early 1930s.

Above the armband, *Sig* rune insignia or diamond-shaped patch of the BDM, all members of the Hitler Youth wore the triangular cloth patch that identified the *Gebiet* and *Obergebiet* to which they belonged. Blue-black or black shoulder straps were in theory worn with both summer and winter uniforms, although these often appear in brown on the summer uniform. The shoulder straps were piped with colours identifying the branch of the HJ to which the *Junge* belonged. For example, those of the *Allgemeine* or 'general' HJ were piped in bright artillery red, while the *Flieger-HJ* had blue, the *Motor-HJ* pink and the *Marine-HJ* yellow. Arabic numerals on the shoulder straps identified the boy's *Gefolgschaft* and *Bann*, and Roman numerals, if carried, his *Unterbann*. Rank was denoted by a system of pips, bars and oak leaves on the shoulder straps. For example, one pip indicated a

This BDM girl wears the popular brown *Kletterjacke* (climbing jacket) over her white shirt and black scarf. Her hair is braided in the officially approved manner, and she wears a black beret. The *Kletterjacke* carries several attainment badges, as well as the Hitler Youth emblem and her *Gebietsdreieck*. (Author's collection)

Kameradschaftsführer, two pips a *Scharführer*, and three a *Gefolgsschaftsführer*, leading 10, 40 and 160 boys respectively. Different coloured lanyards indicated leadership responsibilities, as distinct from rank. A patch on the upper right arm, bearing a system of chevrons and pips, indicated rank in the DJ. The addition of a narrow red cord on the shoulder straps of the HJ identified its wearer as a *Kriegsfreiwilliger* (war volunteer).

Specialist formations of the HJ also had their own distinctive uniforms. For example, the *Marine-HJ* wore uniforms modelled on those of naval cadets, with the addition of HJ insignia. Uniform distinctions such as cuff titles identified those belonging to other special formations such as the *HJ-Streifendienst* (Patrol Service).

During the early years of the war, a field training uniform called an *Arbeitanzug* or *Drillich* was introduced for the HJ. This consisted of a waist-length jacket with two breast pockets and lay-down collar, trousers, black ankle boots with leggings and a side cap. There was considerable variation in the colour of this uniform, from brown, to olive-green, to field grey. The only insignia normally worn with this uniform was the HJ armband, and an HJ badge on the cap. Another specialist uniform that proved popular as a combat uniform in the last months of the war was the M42 HJ *Feurwehr* (fire protection) uniform. This practical and sturdy uniform included a four-pocketed tunic, and was coloured olive-brown.

A *Flakhelfer* poses for a family snapshot. He is wearing the Luftwaffe-grey *Flakhelfer* uniform, modelled on the HJ winter uniform. Although propaganda photographs usually show the HJ armband being worn with the uniform, this was often omitted. (Author's collection)

Combat uniforms

The only specifically combat uniform to be introduced for the HJ was that introduced for the *Flakhelfer* after February 1943. This was similar in cut to the M37 HJ winter uniform, consisting of long trousers and a waist-length blouse with two breast pockets. Headgear consisted of either a peaked cap similar to the M1943 *Einheitsfeldmütze* worn by the infantry or a side cap, and a distinctive greatcoat with two breast pockets was also provided. The uniform was coloured Luftwaffe-grey. The HJ armband and cap insignia were supposed to be worn with this uniform, although many *Flakhelfer* omitted to wear these whenever possible. Instead, many caps unofficially bore a Luftwaffe eagle. A distinctive triangular patch bearing a Luftwaffe eagle was also worn on the right breast, surmounted by the letters 'LH' (*Luftwaffenhelfer*) in Gothic script. Members of the BDM pressed into service as *Flakhelferinnen* towards the end of the war had no uniform of their own, as they were officially not supposed to be performing these duties. Those who did serve probably wore the same uniform that *Flakhelferinnen* over the age of 18 were issued with.

In the final months of the war, many *Luftwaffenhelfer* found themselves pressed into action as ground troops, and generally fought in their distinctive uniforms. Other members of the HJ and DJV found themselves drawn into active combat roles wearing a bewildering variety of uniforms. Mostly, they saw combat as members of the Volkssturm, after its creation on 25 September 1944. The Volkssturm did not have its own uniform, requiring its members to provide themselves with military or party uniforms. The distinguishing insignia of the Volkssturm was nothing more than an armband worn on the left arm, seen in a variety of styles, and bearing the legend *Deutscher Volkssturm – Wehrmacht* in two lines.

Since members of the Hitler Youth did possess their own uniforms, they often presented a more standardized appearance than older members of the Volkssturm, who could be seen wearing a motley collection of civilian clothes, SA or RAD uniforms, and military

There were several different designs of the Volkssturm armband. This *Hitlerjunge* in East Prussia in 1944 wears one of the simplest. (Ullstein)

uniforms of First World War vintage. The greater uniformity of the HJ within the Volkssturm was heightened by the tendency to create separate companies within Volkssturm battalions consisting solely of members of the HJ. Many members of these simply wore their HJ uniforms, or some combination of HJ uniform items. The blue-black M37 winter uniform was often worn, although its colour did not make it the most practical uniform to wear in combat. More suitable were the M42 *Feurwehr* uniform or the field service *Arbeitanzug*. When supplies were available, some HJ units were issued with army uniforms. For example, one *HJ-Nahkampfbrigade* (close fighting brigade) formed at Rothenburg was equipped with stocks of surplus desert uniforms. In practice, members of the HJ, DJV and BDM often equipped themselves as best they could, and variety was the rule. Some eyewitnesses even recall seeing members of the *Jungvolk* fighting in Berlin wearing shorts.

Young Germans called upon to fight within the Volkssturm therefore often did so in a bewildering variety of uniform items. Hugo Stehkämper was conscripted into the Volkssturm in February 1945 at the age of 15, with the intention that he be sent into action against US troops. The uniform with which he was equipped consisted of a pre-war black SS uniform, brown greatcoat belonging to the Organisation Todt, a blue *Flakhelfer* cap and a French helmet. Their appearance was a source of shame to Hugo and his companions – they wanted to fight as German soldiers, not as 'imitation French'.

Many members of the Hitler Youth called up into combat units responded to their new role by trying to make themselves look as 'military' as possible. Hans-Joachim Ullrich gives an interesting account of this. As a 15-year-old leader of a *Jungzug* of the DJV, Hans-Joachim was called upon to assist with the building of fortifications around Breslau. Acutely conscious that this role involved him giving orders to people old enough to be his grandparents, he set out to make himself look as much like a soldier as possible. Hans-Joachim removed all the insignia from his HJ winter uniform, adding a Wehrmacht eagle to his cap until he was told to remove it by the Leutnant supervising the labour work. His attempts to secure grey trousers were unsuccessful, but Hans-Joachim was able to barter cigarettes for some canvas ankle gaiters, and he contrived to cover his HJ tunic by wearing a camouflaged *Zeltbahn* tent section over it.

BELIEF AND BELONGING

Kampfzeit

When Max joined the DJV in 1930, the Hitler Youth organization was at a very exciting stage of its development. The Nazi Party was still outside the political mainstream, battling for legitimacy and power. The sense of belonging to a dynamic, counter-cultural movement involved in a struggle to shape the destiny of Germany was often a profound experience for members of the Hitler Youth before 1933. Although she joined the BDM shortly after Hitler's coming to power, Melita Maschmann writes eloquently of the appeal of the movement for many of her contemporaries: 'I wanted to break out from my childish, narrow life and attach it to something that was great and essential.'

The sense of struggle that was so much a part of the mindset of many members of the Hitler Youth prior to 1933 was not simply a product of empty rhetoric. Often members of the HJ and DJV were involved in street fighting with Communists and Socialists, alongside their older comrades in the SA. The Hitler Youth *Fahnenlied* (banner song) written

Variety is the rule with combat uniforms of the Hitler Youth. The *Junge* in the centre wears a Luftwaffe *Fliegerbluse* tunic. However, his HJ cap bears an army eagle. In addition to the Iron Cross 2nd Class he wears a tank destruction badge on his right sleeve. (Ullstein)

by Schirach had the refrain 'Our banner means more to us than death'. Between 1931 and 1933, 23 members of the Hitler Youth were killed in political violence. Most famously, the 12-year-old *Pimpf* Herbert Norkus was killed and mutilated on 26 January 1932 while posting bills for the Nazi Party in Berlin. Norkus was celebrated as the Hitler Youth martyr par excellence, commemorated in the 1933 film *Hitlerjunge Quex*. For Hitler Youths such as Max, an exact contemporary of Norkus, the death of one of their own gave them a hero to emulate, and a powerful sense of being involved in something significant, dangerous and exciting. This was further emphasized by government attempts to ban the movement prior to 1933. In April 1932 the paramilitary organizations of the Nazi Party were prohibited. This resulted in the Hitler Youth briefly changing its name, until Chancellor Franz von Papen revoked the prohibition against it in June of the same year.

The appeal of the Hitler Youth also drew on deep currents within German culture. In particular, former members of the organization often speak of the attraction of the idea of the *Volksgemeinschaft*, or 'national community'. The Hitler Youth seemed to offer a vision of an ideal community, the members of which would be judged on the basis of their effort and attainment, and not on their wealth or family background. In this sense, the Hitler Youth throughout its history tended to be more egalitarian than other branches of the Nazi state, in that individual status and aspiration were seen as unimportant in comparison to the organic unity of the whole. When marching with his comrades, and especially at huge meetings such as the 1935 Nuremberg Party Rally, Max experienced the almost religious thrill of being caught up in a great mass of people focussed on the same cause.

Another major appeal of the Hitler Youth was that this was an organization for youth led by youth. The idea of 'Youth Leading Youth' was central to Hitler Youth ideology, and was widely reflected in practice. For example, the average age of a *Bannführer* during the 1930s was 24, drastically reduced after 1939. It was rare to find a *Gefolgschaftsführer* older than 17.

The Hitler Youth enters the mainstream

After the excitement of the *Kampfzeit*, many members of the Hitler Youth found the years after 1933 to be something of a disappointment. Max had been deeply involved in election-eering for the party in Rothenburg in the lead-up to the elections of July and November 1932. Along with other members of his *Jungzug* of 50 boys, he took part in defiant marches through the streets, sometimes trading stones and blows with young Communists. He had worked to distribute pamphlets and bills, a job given a particular edge of glamour and danger once news of the death of Herbert Norkus in Berlin was announced. After 1933, however, the Hitler Youth became part of the mainstream, and its ranks swelled with new members who did not share the experience of the years of struggle. Max viewed many of these 'March violets' with contempt, suspecting that most now joined the Hitler Youth because it had become fashionable.

After 1933, therefore, many young Germans viewed the Hitler Youth as part of the mainstream adult world, rather than as a radical alternative to it. The activities of the Hitler Youth as the state youth organization were aimed at indoctrinating its members and preparing them for narrowly defined roles as adults, not at harnessing the idealism of youth to serve a revolutionary goal. Many former members of the Hitler Youth, and especially of the BDM, look back on the 1930s as a dull time. They went through the motions of ideological instruction, drill, sport and communal activities such as singing, but there no longer seemed to be much point to it all.

The outbreak of war changed all this. As the young people of Germany were increasingly relied upon to maintain the war effort, their sense of involvement in something of crucial significance returned. The leadership of the Hitler Youth were fully aware of this, and exploited the desire for significance felt by their young charges to recapture something of the sense of the *Kampfzeit* prior to 1933. Ernst, Maria and Karl were made to feel that their work for the Hitler Youth was playing a small but significant role in Germany's struggle for survival. Ernst and Karl, in particular, eagerly anticipated being able to play their part as soldiers. By 1944, all three of them had experienced the air raids that were turning German cities into rubble, and Maria and Ernst had both lost older brothers in action on the

Girls of the BDM help to raise money in 1939. Their banner reads 'A penny a day to the air defence'. The *Luftschutz* (air defence) was just one organization that made use of the time and enthusiasm of the Hitler Youth. (Ullstein)

Members of the Hitler Youth drafted into the Volkssturm often formed their own distinct units. This *Jungschützenkompanie* (literally 'young marksman's company') was part of the Innsbruck Volkssturm in late 1944. (Ullstein)

Eastern Front. It was understandable in this environment that they succumbed easily to propaganda that both flattered them and demanded greater and greater sacrifices from them. In October 1944, Hitler issued a proclamation to war volunteers born in 1928, in which he urged them to fight fanatically for the Reich against the 'merciless extermination plans of our enemies'. A lifetime of indoctrination coupled with such urgent appeals to save their country in its hour of need influenced many to fight fanatically, while many older soldiers were simply bent on survival. Reinhold Kerstan writes of how proud he felt at the age of 13 in 1945 to be given an armband and 'promoted' to the HJ. Despite being underage, he was told that he was old enough to fight for the Führer. Reinhold's whole life of indoctrination in the Hitler Youth and Nazi school system had prepared him for that moment.

Flakhelfer – neither soldiers nor HJ

As mentioned earlier, the ambiguous position of *Flakhelfer* between the HJ and the Wehrmacht resulted in the development of a distinct *Flakhelfer* identity. Essentially, the use of 15- and 16-year-olds in the air defences of the Reich was an admission that the German war effort could only be maintained through the use of children as soldiers. However, when the scheme was first discussed in early 1943 the Nazi leadership realized that admitting this openly could provoke parental opposition, and would certainly provide Allied propaganda with effective ammunition. It was therefore decided that *Luftwaffenhelfer* should continue to belong to the HJ, wear HJ insignia, and continue to receive school instruction.

Karl's response to this pretence was typical of many other *Flakhelfer*. He saw himself as a soldier, doing the work of a man, and he despised the HJ as civilians whom he had outgrown. He resented having to wear his HJ armband and cap badge, and removed them both whenever possible. Even around the battery where Karl was stationed, his commander usually allowed the *Flakhelfer* to remove their HJ insignia, only expecting it to be worn during formal training and parades. Karl and his friends were involved in a real war. All had seen the effects of Allied bombing raids on their hometowns, and they were motivated by a strong desire to protect their families and get back at the enemies who were attacking them.

Although Karl saw himself as a soldier, he was constantly being reminded that he was not. This had begun during the four weeks of training he had received in March 1944, during which the NCO in charge of Karl's group had ridiculed them as children, and gone out of his way to try to shock them with foul language and smutty jokes. After months of action against Allied bombers, Karl was still aware that he was not a full member of the Wehrmacht, but only a member of the 'Baby

Two *Flakhelfer* practise loading a captured Czech Flak gun in the Ruhr, early 1943. Strenuous tasks such as carrying ammunition and loading large-calibre guns were not officially sanctioned for the teenaged *Flakhelfer*, but were nevertheless often undertaken. (Ralf Blank, Hagen)

**A song of the *Flakhelfer*, played
on German radio in 1943–44.**

Flak' in the eyes of the adults and girls he hoped to impress. There was also often tension between Karl and his mother, who continued to treat him as a child.

One response to this was that Karl and his friends tried to emphasize their military identity. Not only did they neglect to wear their HJ insignia, but they also unofficially replaced it with the Luftwaffe eagle badge on their caps. They sang Wehrmacht songs, no longer the songs of the HJ. But since they were not able to gain full acceptance from the Wehrmacht, the *Flakhelfer* often engaged in small acts of rebellion as a way of asserting an identity of their own. For example, despite it being officially frowned upon by the regime, Karl's barracks listened to jazz and swing records. Karl grew his hair longer than regulations allowed, and he even talked to the Russian POWs at the battery when no Luftwaffe troops were around. Something of this sense that *Flakhelfer* had that they belonged to an exclusive, distinct group is reflected in the lyrics of a song that was played on German radio during 1943–44 (see left).

Opposition to the Hitler Youth

For a small minority of young Germans, the Hitler Youth and its responsibilities were obnoxious. It is misleading to speak of a unified 'resistance' mounted by German youth. Nevertheless, there were a number of groups with very different motivations opposed to the demands placed upon German youth by their leaders.

At one end of the spectrum were the small numbers of young Germans who took a stand against the regime for ideological reasons. The most famous of these were the members of the 'White Rose' group, formed in Munich around Sophie and Hans Scholl. The Hitler Youth credentials of the Scholls were impeccable. Sophie had been a leader in the DJM in the late 1930s, while Hans had carried the flag representing 4,000 Ulm HJ at the Nuremberg Rally in 1935. Despite this background, Hans's experiences on the Russian front had made him an implacable opponent of the Nazi regime by 1942. He and Sophie distributed leaflets in Munich from late 1942 denouncing the regime. They were caught, tried and executed in February 1943.

Less ideologically motivated were a whole range of working-class youth associations and gangs throughout Germany. These groups had little in common with each other apart from a rejection of the Hitler Youth. In the traditionally left-wing Hamburg districts of Altona and Harburg, a loose subculture of proletarian youth mounted attacks on members of the Hitler Youth, and particularly on members of the hated *HJ-Streifendienst*. Also left-leaning were the so-called *Meuten* (mobs) of Leipzig. Other groups, such as the western 'Edelweiss Pirates' were less politically motivated, and owed their inspiration to the thriving youth culture of Weimar Germany.

Another type of youth subculture was the *Swingjugend*, whose members largely belonged to the upper middle class. The *Swingjugend* originated in Hamburg around 1938 and were essentially apolitical aesthetes with a taste for Anglo-American swing music and fashions. The boys advertised their counter-cultural stance through their long hair, crepe-soled shoes and long jackets, while the girls of the *Swingjugend* rejected the official values of the BDM by wearing make-up and nail varnish. The young Germans who identified with the *Swingjugend* may have felt that they were simply interested in having a good time, but in the context of the Third Reich their interests were seen as inherently political. Not only did they seek to opt out of the Nazi plan for German youth embodied in the Hitler Youth, but they idolized music that the Nazi leadership associated with Negroes and Jews, and they welcomed Jews and other 'undesirables' to their dance parties and jam sessions. As late as 1944, the *Swingjugend* were seen as a sufficient threat by Himmler for him to order their brutal suppression, with many of their 'leaders' – some of whom turned out to be also active members of the Hitler Youth – being sent to concentration camps.

Regardless of their motivation, youth who sought to avoid service in the Hitler Youth were treated as dangerous deviants to be crushed ruthlessly. In August 1940 a prison camp for boys aged from 13 to 21 was established at Moringen, near Göttingen, which held 1,400 boys by the end of the war. Boys at the camp were used for slave labour under a brutal regime, and could be conscripted into the army for use in dangerous duties such as mine clearance. A similar camp was set up for girls in June 1942 at Uckermark, near the Ravensbrück concentration camp. Under the direction of the SS, children could be placed directly into these camps without any legal trial.

HJ commanded by a Luftwaffe major, after surrendering to British troops on 30 April 1945. The boys' ages ranged from 13 to 16, and they may have been used as *Flakhelfer* before being committed to ground combat. The fate of child soldiers such as these depended largely on those who commanded them. (IWM BU4893)

Although many members of the Hitler Youth eagerly looked forward to the chance to fight against the enemy after years of preparation, the actual experience of combat was usually a cruel awakening. The experience and fate of young Germans thrown into battle against the Soviet and Western Allies' armies in the final stages of the war often depended on the choices made by the older NCOs and officers who commanded them. These men often bore the responsibility for whether the children under their command were able to quietly return home or move into captivity when resistance was obviously futile, or whether they were sacrificed to no purpose.

Karl

As a *Flakhelfer* close to the western border of Germany in 1944, Karl was frequently in action. Attacks increased in intensity towards the end of the year, as the Anglo-American armies broke out from Normandy in headlong advance across France. Karl's battery often received very little warning of approaching attackers, so everyone was in a constant state of readiness. Not only did the guns have to be ready to fire at RAF heavy bombers during the night and USAAF bomber formations during the day, but there was also the constant danger of sudden attack by low-flying *Jabos* (fighter-bombers), which steadily increased towards the end of 1944. Karl went about his duties in a state of chronic sleep deprivation. Nevertheless, he was determined not to suffer the fate of a former classmate of his who had had a complete nervous breakdown during one raid. The boy had run screaming from his gun position, and was swiftly packed off home. He was lucky – as a 16-year-old *Luftwaffenhelferin* in January 1945, one former member of the BDM recalls that a girl who ran away under fire from her battery was shot.

When an observer spotted an aircraft and sounded the alarm bell, Karl scrambled to his position in the 'B1', the command post that controlled the fire of the six-gun battery. Karl's usual job was to operate part of the *Kommandogerät 40*. This was a fire control computer attached to a stereoscopic range finder. Data concerning the altitude, speed and course of the target aircraft were obtained by the range finder, and then fed into the computer. This calculated the necessary fuse settings, direction and elevation of the guns, and transmitted the information electronically to the battery. In the case of poor visibility, or at night, data were obtained from radar rather than the range finder. Karl was also trained in the use of the *Malsi* Converter, which was located in a bunker next to B1. The *Malsi* was a device that allowed a battery without radar, or one whose radar wasn't working, to obtain data from a neighbouring Flak battery. Although he would have preferred to be assigned to one of the big 88mm Flak guns, Karl found considerable satisfaction in knowing that the guns fired at his direction, and he shared the excitement of the rest of the fire control crew whenever their battery brought down an enemy aircraft.

Karl's post at the *Kommandogerät 40* required his complete concentration, to the extent that he was often only vaguely aware of the action around him. Nevertheless, the stark realities of war were sometimes brought home to him. On one occasion, a defective shell caused the barrel of the 'Caesar' (Number 3) gun of the battery to explode, killing one of Karl's classmates and badly injuring another. More harrowing were the times when the battery itself came under attack. US aircraft sometimes dropped phosphorus bombs on the position to blind it, filling Karl's post with choking smoke. The battery suffered its worst day in September 1944, when low flying *Jabos* pounced on their positions. A direct hit from a bomb killed the entire crew of one of the guns, which included five *Flakhelfer*. Karl was lucky to escape with ringing ears and bruising from debris thrown up by a near miss.

Shortly after this raid, Karl and his fellow *Flakhelfer* were evacuated from the battery as the US troops closed in around Aachen. They were transferred to the Ruhr, and saw duty at several other Flak installations in early 1945. Finally, in March, the guns from Karl's battery were removed to be used at the front as artillery. Surplus crewmen, Karl among them, were sent to an intensive four-day infantry training course at a *Wehrertüchtigungslager*. Karl was enrolled in the Volkssturm, and organized into an 'Alarm' unit with former *Flakhelfer*, boys from the HJ and several BDM girls. In mid-April, the unit was sent to hold a village near Meschede in the Ruhr pocket against a breakthrough by US armour.

Crouching in his hastily dug foxhole, Karl saw US tanks cautiously approaching the village through the morning mist. One of the HJ boys in his unit fired a *Panzerfaust* at the lead tank when it was still too far away, the projectile exploding harmlessly in the road. The US troops then let loose such a volume of machine gun and tank fire against the village that Karl could scarcely raise his head. The boy next to him was killed, and Karl panicked. Nothing he had experienced in the Flak or in training had prepared him for how completely helpless he felt against the steel monsters approaching his position. He managed to crawl towards the relative shelter of a building, losing his rifle along the way. Inside the village, he was struck by a bullet in the leg, and was being patched up by a girl from the BDM when US troops overran their position and captured them both. Karl's first and only experience of infantry combat bore no resemblance to the heroic stories he had been raised on in the DJV, and he was lucky to survive it.

Maria

Maria was captured along with Karl by US troops in the Ruhr pocket in April 1945, shortly after her 17th birthday. It was of course totally against official Nazi policy for a girl of Maria's age to be exposed to frontline

The use of the BDM as medical auxiliaries often brought them into close proximity with the frontline by the end of the war. US troops captured this 15-year-old army auxiliary (*Wehrmachtshelferin*) on the east bank of the Rhine in 1945. She is wearing army uniform with a Red Cross armband. (IWM EA60400)

fighting. Nevertheless, her experience is representative of some of the ways in which girls of the BDM became combatants in 1944–45.

Until 1943, Maria's contribution to the war effort had consisted of the normal sorts of BDM activities: collecting medicinal herbs, assisting with relief work and helping with the distribution of ration cards. However, her world changed in late 1943, after her mother and younger brother were killed during an RAF raid on Cologne. With her father away at the front, Maria's elderly grandmother became her guardian. Maria was devastated by her mother's death, and determined to do all she could to take revenge on her killers. She longed above all to find work in the Flak defences, and to play a part in bringing down British and American bombers.

Unfortunately for Maria, she was too young to be accepted as a *Luftwaffenhelferin* in late 1943 and 1944. Nevertheless, she did what she could by volunteering her time to assist with clerical duties at Luftwaffe administrative offices in Cologne. She also threw herself into BDM activities, leading a *Jungmädelschar* of 50 girls from the DJM. In March 1945, Maria was approached by a Cologne Hitler Youth leader, who asked if she would consider joining a combat unit of HJ within the Volkssturm to help with food preparation and medical support. Maria leapt at the opportunity, and was trained in the use of the *Panzerfaust*, grenades and pistol. Finally, she accompanied her unit of the Volkssturm when it was rushed into action in April, and was captured by US troops while administering first-aid to Karl. Despite all her intentions, she had never fired a shot.

Ernst

In January 1945 Ernst was in a *Wehrertüchtigungslager* outside Berlin. At the completion of his training, Ernst was drafted into the Volkssturm with the rest of his *Schar* of about 40 boys. Most of February was spent in labour work, digging fortifications around Berlin for up to 15 hours a day. In March, Ernst and his comrades were overjoyed to learn that they would at last have the opportunity to fight. The boys of his *Schar* were to become specialist anti-tank troops attached to the HJ-Regiment 'Berlin', officially to be used behind the front lines in the case of a breakthrough by Soviet armour.

Ernst's *Kameradschaft* of ten boys was now redesignated as a *Panzernähbekämpfungstrupp der HJ* ('close-quarter anti-tank squad of the HJ'). The boys were equipped with bicycles, with eight of the boys (including Ernst) using *Panzerfäuste* and two operating an MG34 light machine gun. They also received captured foreign carbines, which made them better equipped than many similar units thrown into action in the last months of the war. It was not unusual for a group of ten or so boys to have nothing but a couple of *Panzerfäuste* and some grenades between them.

In early April 1945, Ernst's unit was ordered to report to the Olympic Stadium in West Berlin with hundreds of other Hitler Youth for deployment. While they waited for orders, Ernst even helped train boys from the DJV as young as ten in the use of the *Panzerfaust*. The children at the Sports Stadium received many visits from Artur Axmann, who regaled them with the story of Leonidas and his 300 Spartans, who had sacrificed themselves heroically against the Persians at the battle of

Thermopylae in 480 BC. Axmann undertook the training and organization of Hitler Youth units largely on his own authority. On 18 April he visited the harassed General Weidling, whom Hitler would appoint as commander of Berlin on the 24th, and offered him the use of 'his' Hitler Youth detachments. Flying into a rage, Weidling refused to use the children, and demanded that Axmann remove them from danger. Despite assurances, he did not do so.

Soviet assault troops began pushing into the suburbs of Berlin on Hitler's birthday, 20 April. Ernst's *Kameradschaft* was sent with other HJ anti-tank units to Neukölln, south-east of the city centre, under the command of a one-armed former army Leutnant. Many other Hitler Youth who had assembled at the Stadium were sent north to hold the bridges over the Havel River in the futile hope that a relief army would reach Berlin. As it turned out, the sacrifice of young German boys at the Havel bridges mainly served the purpose of allowing a number of high

Nazi officials to escape Berlin by that route. Ernst and his comrades were ordered to act as a 'mobile anti-tank reserve' to bolster the defence of Volkssturm and SS units. With them went a group of girls from the BDM to act as support for the HJ 'soldiers'.

Ernst's first experience of battle came on 23 April. A group of Soviet tanks were making a determined effort to push towards the city centre from the district of Köpenick, and Ernst's unit was called on by a hard-pressed group of Volkssturm for support. The Soviet T34s were attacking without infantry support, and Ernst and two other boys were able to find a good position inside a ruined shop. When the first tank had passed their position, Ernst and his companions ran out into the street and fired their *Panzerfäuste*, knocking out the first and second tank in line, before ducking back into the shelter of the buildings. An officer of the Volkssturm who had witnessed their attack clapped the boys on the back when they returned, promising he would recommend them for a medal.

Ernst was elated by his success, but it wasn't to last. On 24 April, a devastating strike by Soviet rockets killed four of Ernst's friends. Two more were killed the following day while attacking Soviet tanks, and Ernst began to realize that it was only a matter of time before his body was reduced to one of the bloody heaps of rags that had become all too familiar to him. He longed to go home, he longed to sleep. Although the idea of deserting occurred to him, he did not want to end his young life hanged from a lamppost by one of the roving groups of military police out looking for 'cowards'. As well as the fear of punishment, Ernst was motivated by a strong desire to defend his home, and especially his family. All the boys with whom he fought had been bombarded with propaganda calling on them to defend their mothers and sisters from the Soviets. The sound of women's screams coming from city blocks captured by Russian troops at night convinced Ernst that this was a duty he had to perform. Surely relief forces were on their way. He only had to hold out a little longer.

By 30 April, only one other boy from Ernst's anti-tank squad was still fighting with him. Any notion that they belonged to a 'mobile anti-tank reserve' had long since vanished. For several days they had been part of an assorted group of Volkssturm, HJ, BDM and a few SS troops, under the command of an SS officer. All of them were weary beyond measure, hungry and short of ammunition. Nevertheless, Ernst had witnessed acts of amazing courage. Using their knowledge of the area, some local boys from the HJ specialized in weaving their way across rooftops to attack Russian troops with grenades. One had even crept up on a sniper and pushed him down into the street. Ernst had also seen girls from the BDM take up arms. One 16-year-old girl had deliberately allowed a tank to roll right over her foxhole before she fired a *Panzerfaust* vertically into it. The explosion had destroyed the tank, but killed her in the process. The Russian tank crews had learned that even Hitler Youths apparently lying dead on the street or in trenches could suddenly come to life and attack them. Ernst watched them driving over positions held by his friends and turning their tanks on the spot, crushing any survivors. Finally, late in the afternoon on 30 April, Ernst was struck by a fragment of a mortar bomb and bled to death in a Berlin street while the battle continued to rage around him. He had no way of knowing that about two hours earlier Hitler had taken his own life.

CONCLUSION

It is a powerful reflection of the moral bankruptcy of Nazi Germany that there was such a widespread acceptance of the use of child soldiers by 1945. The leadership of the Hitler Youth, Artur Axmann in particular, must bear much of the responsibility for enthusiastically championing a policy that saw tens of thousands of young Germans killed or maimed for no purpose. Against this must be weighed the examples of German army personnel who refused to see them sacrificed in this way, from General Weidling directing the defence of Berlin to the many common soldiers who sometimes forcibly restrained members of the Hitler Youth from attacking enemy troops.

For those child soldiers who survived, adjusting to the post-war world was often very difficult. Service in the Hitler Youth forced them into a premature adulthood of sacrifice, exhausting work and often danger. The idealism of German youth was turned to bitterness by defeat, and by the knowledge that they had sacrificed their youth to a brutal and corrupt regime. For many of the survivors of Hitler's children still living today, these wounds are yet to heal.

An Allied photographer hidden in a doorway in Aachen in October 1944 took this powerful image. After wiping her feet on it, an elderly German lady is in the act of spitting on a Hitler Youth flag. (IWM SFC1D)

GLOSSARY

BDM	Bund Deutscher Mädel. The Hitler Youth formation for girls aged 14 to 18.	**NAPOLA**	*Nationalpolitische Erziehungsanstalt*. Elite leadership schools run by the SS.
DJM	Deutsche Jungmädel. The Hitler Youth formation for girls aged 10 to 14.	**NSDAP**	Nationalsozialistische Deutsche Arbeiterpartei. The Nazi Party.
DJV	Deutsches Jungvolk. The Hitler Youth formation for boys aged 10 to 14.	***Panzerfaust***	Literally 'tank fist'. A disposable, recoilless anti-tank weapon.
Gau	An administrative region of the Nazi Party, led by a *Gauleiter*, responsible for the government of the region.	***Pimpf***	Literally a 'lad'. A member of the DJV.
		RAD	Reichsarbeitsdienst. Compulsory labour service performed after leaving the Hitler Youth at 18.
Gebiet	An administrative region of the Hitler Youth, corresponding to a *Gau* of the Nazi Party.		
Gebietsdreieck	Triangular shoulder patch showing the region to which the Hitler Youth belonged.	**SA**	Sturmabteilung. Nazi paramilitary 'Brownshirts' or 'stormtroopers'.
Hitlerjunge	A member of the HJ.	**SS-VT**	SS-Verfügungstruppe. Literally 'Special Duty Troops' – the original name of the Waffen-SS.
HJ	Hitler Jugend. The Hitler Youth formation for boys aged 14 to 18. Also the name of the whole organization.	***Volksgemeinschaft***	
			'National Community'.
Jabo	German army slang for a *Jagdbomber*, a fighter-bomber aircraft.	**Volkssturm**	Literally 'People's Assault'. German militia force formed in September 1944.
KLV	*Kinderlandverschickung*. An evacuation programme to remove children from cities under air attack.	**Waffen-SS**	'Armed SS'. The SS military formations.
		Wehrertüchtigungslager	
			Literally 'Military service competency camp'. Pre-military training facility for the Hitler Youth.
Landdienst	Agricultural service performed as a Hitler Youth activity.	**Wehrmacht**	German armed forces, as distinct from the Waffen-SS.

BIBLIOGRAPHY

Memoirs

Granzow, K., *Tagbuch eines Hitlerjungen*, Bremen (1965)

Heck, A., *The Burden of Hitler's Legacy*, Frederick (1988)

Kerstan, R., *Blood and Honour*, Tring (1983)

Lehmann, A.D., *In Hitler's Bunker*, Sydney (2003)

Maschmann, M., *Account Rendered: A Dossier on My Former Self*, London (1964)

Metelmann, H., *A Hitler Youth*, Staplehurst (1997)

Steinhoff, J., P. Pechel and D. Showalter, (eds), *Voices from the Third Reich: An Oral History*, Washington DC (1989)

Secondary sources

Angolia, J.R., *The HJ*, San Jose (1991–92)

Baker, P., *Youth Led by Youth*, Doncaster (1989–97)

Beevor, A., *Berlin: The Downfall 1945*, London (2002)

Holzträger, H., *In a Raging Inferno: Combat Units of the Hitler Youth 1944–45*, Solihull (2000)

Itschert, E.A. (et al.), *'Feuer frei – Kinder!' Ein mißbrauchte Generation: Flakhelfer im Einsatz*, Saarbrücken (1984)

Kater, M.H., *Hitler Youth*, Cambridge MA (2004)

Knopp, G., *Hitler's Children*, Stroud (2002)

Koch, H.W., *The Hitler Youth: Origins and Development 1922–1945*, New York (1975)

Lewis, B.R., *Hitler Youth: The Hitlerjugend in War and Peace 1933–45*, Staplehurst (2000)

Meyer, H., *The History of the 12.SS Panzerdivision 'Hitlerjugend'*, Fedorowicz (1994)

Müller, W., *Sound Locators, Fire Control Systems and Searchlights of the German Heavy Flak Units 1939–1945*, Atglen (1998)

Nicolaisen, H.-D., *Die Flakhelfer: Luftwaffenhelfer und Marinehelfer im Zweiten Weltkrieg*, Berlin (1981)

Nicolaisen, H.-D., *Der Einsatz der Luftwaffen- und Marinehelfer im 2. Weltkrieg: Darstellung und Dokumentation*, Bürsum (1981)

Noakes, J. and Pridham, G. (eds), *Nazism 1919–1945: A Documentary Reader. Vol. 2: State, Economy and Society 1933–1939*, Exeter (1984)

Noakes, J. (ed.), *Nazism 1919–1945: A Documentary Reader. Vol. 4: The German Home Front in World War II*, Exeter (1998)

Owings, A., *Frauen: German Women Recall the Third Reich*, London (1993)

Rempel, G., *Hitler's Children: the Hitler Youth and the SS*, Chapel Hill/London (1989)

Ryan, C., *The Last Battle*, London (1966)

Stephens, F.J., *Hitler Youth: History, Organisation, Uniforms and Insignia*, London (1973)

Westerman, E.B., *Flak: German Anti-Aircraft Defences 1914–1945*, Lawrence KS (2001)

COLOUR PLATE COMMENTARY

A: HJ SPORTS, SUMMER 1938
In 1938, at the age of 17, Max was put in charge of a *Gefolgschaft* of 150 boys in his home town of Rothenburg. He is shown here leading them in exercises with an 'Indian club', which strongly resembled the German hand grenade. Max wears the standard summer HJ uniform of brown shirt with black shorts and scarf. His rank as a *Gefolgschaftsführer* is shown by the three silver pips on his shoulder strap, and his leadership function by the lanyard. It was common for HJ leaders to be put in charge of units larger than their rank indicated, especially during the war. Max belongs to the 308th *Bann*, and the triangular patch on his left arm (*Gebietsdreieck*) identifies him as belonging to the *Gebiet* Franken in the Süd (south) *Obergebiet*.

Also shown is a detail of the Hitler Youth belt buckle **(1)** and dagger **(2)**. This was designed to resemble an army bayonet, and bore the inscription 'Blood and Honour'. Max wears a proficiency badge **(3)** and marksmanship badge **(4)**. Proficiency badges awarded to the DJV incorporated the formation's *Sig* rune **(5)**. Two other *Gebiet* patches are shown: one from the BDM, which used white lettering, **(6)**, and a *Traditionsarmdreieck* with gold bar (silver for the BDM) **(7)**. This showed that the wearer's *Bann* had been formed prior to 1933.

B: TRAINING IN A *WEHRERTÜCHTIGUNGSLAGER*, JANUARY 1945
Ernst was ordered to report for a three-week training course at a *Wehrertüchtigungslager* in January 1945, when he was still only 15 years old. At this stage of the war, the instructors at the camp were aware that the boys they were training were likely to be used in combat in a matter of weeks. Here Ernst is receiving instruction in the use of a *Panzerfaust 60*. He is wearing his standard winter HJ uniform, although fatigue uniforms were also commonly worn in the camp. The red cord on Ernst's shoulder strap identifies him as a *Kriegsfreiwillige*, or 'war volunteer', although in reality he had no say in the matter. His instructor is an experienced SS-Unterscharführer (sergeant) from the Leibstandarte Division, seconded to training at the *Wehrertüchtigungslager* while he recovers from a wound.

The *Panzerfaust* was a simple, cheap and effective weapon, but its back-blast made it potentially lethal to the firer if fired from an enclosed space. It fired a rocket-propelled grenade with a hollow-charge warhead, similar in principle to the US Bazooka and the British PIAT. After striking its target, the shaped charge in the warhead **(1)** directed the force of the explosion inwards **(2)**, punching a concentrated jet of molten metal and gas through the armour plating of the tank **(3)**. Successive improvements to the *Panzerfaust* after its introduction in 1943 boosted its effective range to from 30 metres to 60 and then 100 metres (approximately 33 yards to 66 to 110 yards).

C: *LUFTWAFFENHELFER* AT A FLAK INSTALLATION, MARCH 1944
The Flak battery where Karl was stationed as a *Luftwaffenhelfer* from March 1944 conformed to a typical layout. The 'brain' of the battery was its fire control system, known as 'B1' **(1)**. This was usually positioned about 100 metres (110 yards) from the guns themselves. When visibility allowed, crewmen used the long Em 4m R40 stereoscopic range finder to find out a target aircraft's altitude, speed and course. This information was then fed into the *Kommandogerät 40 (Kdo. Ger. 40)*, a fire control computer, which appears as a large box directly in front of the range finder. Karl is here having his calculations checked by a Luftwaffe Unteroffizier (sergeant). As they will shortly be inspected by the battery chief, the boys are wearing correct *HJ-Luftwaffenhelfer* uniforms, including the despised HJ armbands.

At night, or in poor visibility, data for the *Kdo. Ger. 40* could be obtained from the *Würzburg* radar positioned close to B1 **(2)**, which bears the silhouettes of enemy aircraft the battery is credited with downing. A *Malsi* device is also situated in a bunker close by B1, which enables nearby radar to supply the battery with data if their own is damaged. Once the *Kdo. Ger. 40* receives the necessary information about the target aircraft, Karl and a second crewman use the computer to calculate the necessary elevation and fuse settings for the guns, information that is then transmitted to the firing positions

Every Allied and Soviet tank crew feared the well-hidden HJ with a *Panzerfaust*. This HJ, armed with a *Panzerfaust 60*, was photographed during the battle for Berlin. (Ullstein)

Flakhelfer were often entrusted with fire control equipment. This *Würzburg* radar, photographed with its crew near Hagen-Boele in March 1944, was used to direct the fire of a Flak battery at night or in poor visibility. (Ralf Blank, Hagen)

(3). The battery here consists of six 88mm guns, which are protected by individual blast barriers.

D: BDM GIRLS JOIN A SEARCHLIGHT CREW NEAR BERLIN, AUTUMN 1944

Searchlights, or *Flakscheinwerfer*, formed an important part of the anti-aircraft defences of the Reich. Not only did they help Flak artillery and night-fighters to find their targets, but their dazzle could reduce the accuracy of enemy bombing. As a compliment to their effectiveness, Allied aircraft often targeted searchlights. Although Nazi attitudes towards the proper role of women precluded their employment in gun batteries until the final months of the war, *Flakhelferinnen* were crewing searchlights from at least 1943.

Shown here is a 150cm *Flakscheinwerfer 34* in action outside Berlin in autumn 1944. Two members of the crew are 17-year-old volunteers from the BDM. Unlike their male equivalents in the HJ, girls from the BDM were not officially supposed to be serving as anti-aircraft auxiliaries, and had no uniform of their own. Instead, they wear the same *Flakhelferin* uniform as their older colleagues. Their searchlight is part of a battery of 16.

The *Flakscheinwerfer 34* was able to cast a beam to about 12,000 metres ($7\frac{1}{2}$ miles). Some batteries made use of a more powerful 200cm master searchlight, sometimes guided by radar, to direct the rest of the battery to their target.

E: HITLER YOUTH IN THE *LUFTSCHUTZ*, KÖLN, 1943

The *Luftschutz-HJ* was set up in 1939 as a specialist Hitler Youth formation to train its members in air-raid procedures. However, by summer 1942, all members of the Hitler Youth received air-raid training as a matter of course. As the British and US raids against German cities grew in intensity through 1942–43, members of the Hitler Youth of all ages were called upon to fulfil a wide range of medical, welfare, communications and fire-fighting roles. Here, the centre of Köln burns during an RAF night raid in late 1943. Two 17-year-old members of an *HJ-Feuerwehr* (fire defence) squad struggle against the flames. Local city fire brigades trained specialized squads like this, and a distinctive uniform was introduced for them, as worn here. In the foreground is a 17-year-old BDM girl who is training with the Deutsches Rotes Kreuz (German Red Cross) to become a nurse. She works shifts at a Köln hospital, helping with the treatment of wounded soldiers, but is also a volunteer nurse in the *Luftschutz*. She has fitted herself out with a privately purchased boiler suit and 'Gladiator'-style *Luftschutz* helmet, although the gas mask has been issued to her. She has just been told by a 14-year-old HJ messenger that some injured people have been found in the next street who need her help. He has been issued with a vintage M1916 helmet from the First World War and a gas mask, but otherwise wears his normal summer uniform.

F: THE HJ DIVISION COUNTERATTACKS NEAR CAEN, JUNE 1944

Normandy 1944. On the morning of 7 June, the day after the landing of Commonwealth and US troops, elements of the 12th SS-Panzer Division 'Hitler Jugend' were concentrated just to the west of Caen. Canadian armour was pushing south from the invasion beaches when the 'Hitler Jugend' sprang an ambush and launched a frantic counterattack. Panzer IVs from the II.Abteilung (Battalion) of the Division's Panzer Regiment, along with *Panzergrenadiers*, captured the villages of Authie and Franqueville on their first rush, the Allies being taken completely by surprise. Pushing on further north, the elated troops felt they were on the point of breaking through to the sea, but a dangerously exposed flank caused them to be pulled back.

Max is shown here during the attack, pointing out some enemy infantry positions to the commander of a Panzer IV. Max is now a 24-year-old *Hauptsturmführer* (captain) in command of a company of *Panzergrenadiers*. Along with the rest of his men, he wears an M43 SS pattern camouflage smock over his field-grey uniform. In keeping with the ethos of the Hitler Jugend, and the close relationship between officers and men, he is leading from the front. In the foreground, an MG42 team is relocating. The formidable rate of fire of this weapon made ammunition supply a constant problem, so these soldiers have festooned themselves with extra belts, and one carries an additional box of ammunition.

The heady success of the 'Hitler Jugend' Division's first attack was not to last. The division was ground down over the following weeks in vicious defensive fighting without relief. Max was killed in early July by a British artillery barrage.

G: CHILD SOLDIERS IN THE VOLKSSTURM, RUHR POCKET, APRIL 1945

The 'Hitler Jugend' Division went into action as a well-trained and equipped fighting force. In contrast, the members of the Hitler Youth committed to battle as part of the Volkssturm were often highly motivated, but usually no match for the enemy troops they were pitted against. Karl and Maria are shown here shortly before being captured by US troops in the Ruhr pocket in April 1945. After the guns from Karl's Flak battery had been taken to be used as ground artillery, he and other superfluous *Flakhelfer* from the fire control crews had been enrolled in the Volkssturm and given a four-day crash course in infantry weapons at a *Wehrertüchtigungslager*. In March 1945, the Allies crossed the Rhine, and Karl was assigned to an 'Alarm' unit to help prevent a breakthrough. Equipment was hastily provided from a variety of sources. Over his *Flakhelfer* uniform, Karl is wearing a brown greatcoat from RAD stores with a Volkssturm armband. Protecting his head is a captured French army helmet with its national insignia removed. Before being recycled by the Volkssturm, this helmet had been used by a HJ *Luftschutz* squad in Köln, one of whom painted the Hitler Youth insignia

on its side. Karl has been hit by a bullet in the leg, and is receiving treatment from Maria. Thanks to Maria's clerical work for the Luftwaffe in Köln, she was able to gain access to items of *Luftwaffenhelferin* uniform. Over her tunic, trousers and cap issued to female auxiliaries she wears the distinctive *Flakhelfer* greatcoat with breast pockets, which was issued to male HJ auxiliaries. She has unofficially received training in the use of the *Panzerfaust 30* that she is carrying across her back.

H: ERNST PREPARES TO DEFEND BERLIN, APRIL 1945

A few short months after his training at a *Wehrertüchtigungslager*, Ernst has been committed to the desperate battle for Berlin in late April 1945. He has been assigned to an HJ 'anti-tank reserve' unit within the Volkssturm. In practice, this means that he has been issued with a civilian bicycle with two *Panzerfäuste 60* attached. Close by the Olympic Stadium south-west of the city centre, with Soviet artillery sounding clearly in the distance, Ernst waits for orders.

Perhaps in response to his nervousness at the coming ordeal, Ernst has attempted to give himself as military an appearance as possible. He has removed all his HJ insignia from his blue-black winter uniform, and has added whatever military equipment he has been able to find. He wears an army splinter-pattern camouflage smock issued to him from stocks within Berlin, over which he wears his HJ belt and dagger. His single set of ammunition pouches contains only four clips of bullets for the ex-Soviet Moisin-Nagant M38 carbine he carries. Ernst has not yet been able to secure a helmet, and continues to wear his HJ ski cap.

A Soviet cameraman took this photograph of some of the young defenders of Berlin in late April 1945. Most look to be members of the DJV, rather than the HJ, and wear an assortment of fatigue uniforms, some still wearing their Hitler Youth caps. (Stavka)

INDEX